SAN FRANCISCO
Entertains

A Cookbook Celebrating the Centennial
of The Junior League of San Francisco, Inc.

SAN FRANCISCO
Entertains

A Cookbook Celebrating the Centennial
of The Junior League of San Francisco, Inc.

Published by The Junior League of San Francisco, Inc.
Copyright © 2011 by
The Junior League of San Francisco, Inc.
2226A Fillmore Street
San Francisco, California 94115
415-775-4100

Cover and Food Photography © by Lara Hata
Chapter Opener Photography © by Liza Gershman
Location Photography © by Matthew Washburn

This cookbook is a collection of our favorite recipes, which are not necessarily original recipes.

Library of Congress Control Number: 2010927651
ISBN: 978-0-615-29503-9

Edited, Designed, and Produced by

 Favorite Recipes® Press

An imprint of

FRP. INC

A wholly owned subsidiary of Southwestern/Great American, Inc.
P.O. Box 305142
Nashville, Tennessee 37230
800-358-0560

Art Director and Book Design: Steve Newman
Project Editor: Tanis Westbrook

Manufactured in the United States of America
First Printing: 2011
10,000 copies

Photography

MATTHEW WASHBURN, *Iconic San Francisco Photographer*

Photography and Music. The idea that these two are closely related is unexpected. Music exists as sound over time and photographs exist as light without time. Matthew Washburn pursues them both.

Matthew studied music at the University of the Pacific in Stockton. During his final semester at UOP, Matthew found he had an interest in photography. He arrived for graduate school at the San Francisco Conservatory of Music and spent the summer exploring the city with his camera. Eventually, he began photographing fellow students at the Conservatory. Since then, Matthew's made a career of photography. washburnimagery.com

LIZA GERSHMAN, *Chapter Opener Photographer*

Liza Gershman is an award-winning photographer and freelance writer who happily splits her time between San Francisco and Napa Valley, when she is not traipsing across the globe. Her work has been featured in publications such as the *San Francisco Chronicle, Outside Magazine, 7x7* magazine, and *Napa Valley Life* magazine. Most recently, Liza finished photographing a book for Random House on absinthe cocktails. lizagershman.com

LARA HATA, *Food Photographer*

Photographer Lara Hata lives, works, and eats in the San Francisco Bay Area. Lara specializes in food photography and loves setting her professional life amidst all the joys and comforts of the kitchen. larahata.com

Alexa Hyman, *Food Stylist*
Jeff Larson, *Food Styling Assistant*
Carol Hacker, *Prop Stylist*
Ha Huynh, *First Assistant*
Josephine Leung, *Assistant*

FOR FOOD PHOTOGRAPHY LOCATIONS, THANKS TO

The Massocca Family
Matthew Paige
Millennium Tower, San Francisco

Mission

The Junior League of San Francisco, Inc., (JLSF) is an organization of women committed to promoting voluntarism, developing the potential of women, and improving communities through the effective action and leadership of trained volunteers. Its purpose is exclusively educational and charitable.

Since its inception in 1911, the Junior League of San Francisco, Inc., has provided the community with an estimated seven million volunteer hours and more than $24 million through direct community grants, advocacy, and membership training and development.

As a problem surfaces within the community, the JLSF is frequently the first organization to recognize and address the issue, providing volunteer energy, financial assistance, and public support. Often in collaboration with other community groups and/or the public sector, the JLSF designs and launches a program, then works to achieve community impact and measurable results.

The Junior League of San Francisco

A member of The Association of Junior Leagues International, Inc.

Women building better communities

Foreword

CHEF GARY DANKO, *Restaurant Gary Danko*

Entertaining in the San Francisco Bay Area is no joke. As signaled by the astonishing number of great restaurants, farmers' markets, and exquisite food shops here, the Bay Area is home to one of the most passionate and appreciative foodie cultures in the world. For lots of people here, every meal, every snack, is the subject of thoughtful consideration. This is to say people here do not partake lightly in the culture of food and wine—we live and die for it. And that's a beautiful thing.

As someone who has cooked my entire life—most of it in a professional restaurant kitchen—I must confess that my greatest personal pleasure comes from entertaining at home. A good dinner party fosters a shared energy, a connection between host and guest, which is very different than a restaurant experience. I love the ritual of setting a beautiful table, finding the perfect flowers, mixing a perfect drink, and preparing the appropriate dishes for the season and the occasion. As anyone who regularly entertains knows, a lot of work goes into pulling off a great party. Ideas, recipes, and tips from seasoned hosts are always welcome. And that's the value of this book.

San Francisco Entertains shares recipes from both local professional chefs and some of the insatiable foodies that live here. It's a foodie's manual for the perfect party. Rest assured, these tried-and-true recipes will please even the most discerning palates, be it at a relaxed family gathering, a charged dinner party for your partner's boss, or simply an impromptu get-together. And the book is very San Francisco, embracing the bounty of foods produced around here as well as capturing the style and spirit of the way we as a food culture like to eat. Best of all, the recipes are easy to follow and use ingredients that are not hard to find. Even if you're cooking for the most die-hard and experienced of Bay Area—something that I seem to do every day of my life!—the number one thing to remember is that entertaining at home doesn't need to be complicated or stressful, just fun.

Contents

Contents

Menus

COZY VALENTINE'S DAY SUPPER FOR TWO

Pear Flower Martini
Oyster Mignonette
Rack of Lamb with Pistachio Mint Pesto
Tarragon Green Beans
Garlic and Herb Tomatoes
Molten Lava Chocolate Cupcakes
Irish Coffee for Two

CHINESE NEW YEAR DRAGON CELEBRATION

Ginger Crab Rolls
Hoisin Stir-Fried Chicken
Brown Rice *
Fortune Cookies and Mandarin Oranges *
Green Tea *

NORTH BEACH ITALIAN FAMILY GET-TOGETHER

Red Wine *
California Cioppino
Boudin Bakery Sourdough Bread *
Green Salad with Italian Vinaigrette *
North Beach Tiramisu
Espresso *

Items marked with an * are suggestions. Purchase at the store or use your favorite recipe.

Menus

CINCO DE MAYO FIESTA

Mission Margaritas

Wine Country Guacamole with Jicama Sticks

Red Snapper Ceviche with Green Apple

Fish Tacos with Tomato-Mango Salsa

Green Salad with Mexican Vinaigrette

Ancho Chile Brownies

OPENING DAY ON THE BAY BREAKFAST

Sparkling Fogcutter

Open-Face Italian Sausage Omelet

Cable Car Morning Muffins

Coffee and Fresh-Squeezed Orange Juice *

MOTHER'S DAY BRUNCH

Chai Tea Latte

Asparagus and Roasted Red Pepper Strata

Creamy Grits with Apple and Pancetta

Fruit Pizza

SUMMER AFTERNOON GRILL PARTY

Crisp Sauvignon Blanc *

White Bean Dip with Toasted Pita

Heirloom Tomato Gazpacho

Grilled Fish with Lemon Caper Sauce

Summer Corn Salad

Meyer Lemon Ice Cream

Menus

49ers Football Tailgate

Samuel Adams Octoberfest Beer *
Prosciutto and Sage Pinwheels
Turkey Chili
Corn Bread *
Indian Spinach Salad
Chocolate and Peanut Butter Squares

Wine Country Cocktail Party

Red and White Wine *
Tuna Tartare
Pesto and Goat Cheese Tarts
Fig and Blue Cheese Poppers
Spiced Beef Phyllo Cups with Mint and Feta
Roasted Nuts and Assorted Olives *
Seasonal Fresh Fruit *

Foggy Day/Baby It's Cold Outside Winter Meal

Hot Spiced Wine
Mushroom Pâté with Pickled Red Onion Confit
Drunken Crab Soup
Chicken Provençal
Roasted Baby Red Potatoes
Baked Goat Cheese Salad
Chocolate Macadamia Nut Pie

Menus

THANKSGIVING TRIMMINGS
(ALL YOU NEED IS THE TURKEY)

Red and White Wine *

Cranberry Brie

Rosemary–Brown Sugar Cashews

Curried Butternut Squash Soup

Roasted Turkey with Cranberry Merlot Sauce

Sourdough and Fennel Stuffing

Brussels Sprouts with Crispy Pancetta

Apple Crisp with Whipped Cream

Coffee and Tea *

WINTER SOLSTICE DINNER

Gloria Ferrier Sonoma Brut Sparkling Wine *

Smoked Salmon Wontons with Wasabi Sauce

Buckwheat Blini with Osetra Caviar

Pancetta-Studded Beef Tenderloin

Roasted Cauliflower and Walnuts

Green Salad with Green Goddess Salad Dressing

Triple-Chip Cookies

Vanilla Ice Cream *

Coffee and Tea *

Items marked with an * are suggestions. Purchase at the store or use your favorite recipe.

Beverages

The year 1911 saw the historic granting of women's suffrage rights in California—and the founding of The Junior League of San Francisco, Inc., (JLSF). The JLSF's first meeting was held at the Otis home, located at 2231 Broadway, San Francisco. In attendance were Gertrude Creswell, Augusta Foute, Ethel McAllister, Cora Otis, Fredericka Otis, Cora Smith, Gertrude Thomas, and Dora Winn (president). They planned *Under Cover*, the JLSF's first play and fundraiser that garnered $900, which was used to establish paying work spaces for unemployed women. Of even greater note, in 1917 JLSF volunteers formed the Motor Delivery Service, driving nurses, doctors, patients, and supplies between hospital wards during the major influenza pandemic outbreak that year. This emergency medical transportation model formed the prototype for the national organization Red Cross Motor Corps.

In the culinary world, the specter of Prohibition influenced drinking customs in the twentieth century's first decades. Hosts greeted dinner party guests with fashionable fruit cocktails consisting of frozen fruit juices sweetened with sugar. These water ices titillated palates as latter-day *amuse-bouche* before the start of decadent seven-course meals. While Prohibition did cast its shadow, the alcohol ban lasted only fourteen years, leaving San Francisco ample time to develop a vibrant cocktail culture. Among the City by the Bay's more famous alcoholic cocktails, it is rumored that the martini originated during the Gold Rush era, and it is documented that the Bank Exchange invented Pisco Punch around the turn of the century. (Later in the century, San Francisco would popularize Irish coffee and the Mai Tai.) In 1910, nationally renowned mixologist "Cocktail Bill" Boothby served up his namesake Boothby Cocktail at the Palace Hotel bar, the hotel itself just returned to splendor after the devastation of the 1906 earthquake.

San Francisco witnessed massive rebuilding in the 1910s in preparation to host the 1915 Panama-Pacific International Exposition. The World's Fair, as the exposition was also known, would allow the recovering city to celebrate the opening of the Panama Canal, showcase its resurrection from the earthquake, and ascend to international prominence in science and industry. The beginning of the decade saw the San Francisco Bay dredged to provide sand for the Fair's home in the new Harbor View district (now known as the Marina), the construction of the iconic Palace of Fine Arts, and, in the Civic Center neighborhood, the Beaux-Arts City Hall and Main Library.

1911–1920

PISCO PUNCH

Courtesy of Oola Restaurant and Bar

SERVES 1

2 ounces Pisco
1 ounce distilled water
3/4 ounce pineapple gum syrup

3/4 ounce lemon juice
Pineapple wedges for
 garnish

Special Equipment: *cocktail shaker*

Combine the ingredients in an ice-filled cocktail shaker. Shake for 10 to 15 seconds. Strain into a chilled punch glass. Garnish with a pineapple wedge that has been soaked overnight in the gum syrup.

KIWI CUCUMBER COCKTAIL

SERVES 2

8 seedless green grapes
1 kiwifruit, peeled and sliced
6 peeled cucumber slices
6 basil leaves

3 ounces (6 tablespoons)
 Blue Angel vodka
3/4 cup lemonade
2 tablespoons simple syrup

Special Equipment: *cocktail shaker, muddler*

Place the grapes, kiwifruit, cucumber and basil in a cocktail shaker. Use a muddler to crush the mixture. Add the vodka, lemonade and simple syrup; fill with ice cubes and shake well. Strain into highball glasses.

CHEF'S TIP: If you do not have a muddler, you can use a wooden spoon or the back of a large silver spoon, pressing the ingredients to release the flavor.

Sugar Pumpkin Martini

SERVES 10

Pumpkin Vodka
1 liter vanilla vodka
2 cups roasted sugar pumpkin (below)
2 tablespoons pumpkin pie spice

Sugar Pumpkin Martini
Cinnamon and sugar to taste
1 quart half-and-half
10 tablespoons simple syrup
Cinnamon, for garnish

Special Equipment: *cheesecloth, cocktail shaker*

Vodka
Pour the vodka into a large pitcher or container with a tightly fitting lid, reserving the empty vodka bottle. Add the roasted pumpkin and pumpkin pie spice to the pitcher and shake to mix well. Chill in the refrigerator for 2 days. Strain through a cheesecloth into the reserved bottle. Store in the refrigerator for up to 3 weeks.

Martini
For each martini, dampen the rim of a martini glass and dip into a mixture of cinnamon and sugar. Combine 1 1/2 ounces of the pumpkin vodka, 1 1/2 ounces of the half-and-half and ice in a shaker and add 1 tablespoon of the simple syrup. Shake and strain into the prepared martini glass. Garnish with a sprinkle of additional cinnamon.

Roasted Pumpkin

Cut a sugar pumpkin into halves and discard the seeds. Peel with a vegetable peeler and cut into 1-inch cubes. Spread on a rimmed baking sheet coated with olive oil or butter. Roast at 400 degrees for 20 to 25 minutes or until tender, stirring after 10 minutes.

Pear Flower Martini

SERVES 2

3 ounces (6 tablespoons) elderflower liqueur
2 ounces (1/4 cup) gin
2 ounces (1/4 cup) pear vodka
Sparkling wine
Pear juice, optional

Special Equipment: *cocktail shaker*

Pour the elderflower liqueur, gin and vodka into a cocktail shaker with ice and shake until cold. Strain into chilled martini glasses and top with a splash of sparkling wine. If it's too strong, add a splash of pear juice.

The Martini

A triumphant Gold Rush miner is said to have asked for Champagne and instead was served the bartender's "special"—a cocktail made of gin and vermouth named after the Bay Area town of Martinez.

Lavender Raspberry Lemonade

SERVES 8

1/4 cup food-grade lavender flowers
1 cup boiling water
1 pint raspberries
3 cups boiling water
Juice of 2 large or 3 small lemons
2 tablespoons honey
2 to 3 tablespoons sugar
12 ounces (1 1/2 cups) Blue Angel vodka
Additional sugar

Special Equipment: *fine mesh sieve*

Combine the lavender flowers with 1 cup boiling water in a small bowl. Cover and let stand for 10 minutes.

Mash the raspberries in a bowl. Spoon into a fine mesh sieve over a bowl and pour 3 cups boiling water over the raspberries; discard the seeds. Strain the lemon juice and lavender water into the raspberries, reserving the juiced lemons. Stir in the honey and 2 to 3 tablespoons sugar until completely dissolved. Chill in the refrigerator.

Dampen the rims of cocktail glasses with the reserved lemons and dip in additional sugar. Fill the glasses with ice and add 3 tablespoons vodka to each glass. Fill with the raspberry lemonade and serve.

THIS PAGE GRACIOUSLY SPONSORED BY WENDY SIMON ARMSTRONG & BENTON ARMSTRONG

SPARKLING WINE MOJITO

SERVES 6

1 cup mint leaves, julienned
2/3 cup lime juice
1 (750-milliliter) bottle sparkling wine, chilled

Special Equipment: *muddler*

Muddle the mint leaves and lime juice in a large pitcher. Add the wine and mix gently. Strain into glasses and serve immediately.

Know the Language

- Proof refers to the alcohol content. One hundred-proof liquor has a 50% alcohol content.
- "Neat" means served straight out of the bottle, without water, mixers, or ice.
- "Straight up" or "Up" refers to a drink shaken or stirred with ice before being strained into a glass without ice.
- "On the rocks" means served over ice.

BLUEBERRY MOJITO

A great summer drink for a backyard barbecue or an alternative to a mimosa.

SERVES 1

1/2 cup fresh blueberries
1 tablespoon superfine sugar
Juice of 1/2 lime
12 to 15 fresh mint leaves
1 1/2 ounces (3 tablespoons) white rum
1/4 cup club soda
1/2 cup ice
Blueberries and mint leaves, for garnish

Special Equipment: *muddler*

Mix 1/2 cup blueberries with the sugar, lime juice and mint leaves in a tall glass. Muddle until the berries and mint are combined and the flavors mix. Place in a serving glass and add the rum, club soda and ice; stir to mix well. Garnish with additional blueberries and a mint leaf.

SPARKLING FOGCUTTER

A simple brunch cocktail to perk up a foggy summer day in San Francisco.

SERVES 6

8 ounces whole strawberries
1 tablespoon sugar, or to taste
1 (750-milliliter) bottle sparkling wine, chilled

Special Equipment: *fine mesh sieve*

Purée the strawberries in a blender. Strain through a fine mesh sieve into a small bowl, discarding the pulp and seeds. Stir in the sugar until dissolved. Place 1 tablespoon of the purée in each champagne glass and fill with the sparkling wine; stir gently.

CHEF'S TIP: Substitute other seasonal fruit for the strawberries. Watermelon is a delicious option.

STRAWBERRY FIELDS

Courtesy of The Tipsy Pig

SERVES 1

2 or 3 strawberries, chopped
2 ounces (1/4 cup) vodka
Juice of 1 lime
2 tablespoons simple syrup
Soda water
Lime wedge, for garnish

Special Equipment: *muddler*

Muddle the strawberries almost to a purée in a 10-ounce cocktail glass. Stir in the vodka, lime juice and simple syrup. Fill with ice and add soda water; mix gently. Garnish with a lime wedge.

The Popsicle

The popsicle was invented in San Francisco by 11-year-old Frank Epperson in 1905. While typically a delicious snack for children, freeze a fruit-flavored cocktail for a fun adult treat!

THIS PAGE GRACIOUSLY SPONSORED BY AMANDA WILLSON

MISSION MARGARITAS

SERVES 4

1¹/2 cups blue agave tequila
¹/2 cup orange liqueur
1 (12-ounce) can frozen lemonade concentrate
4 ounces (¹/2 cup) domestic beer
Juice of 1 lemon
Juice of 1 lime
1 tablespoon sugar, or to taste

Combine the tequila, orange liqueur, lemonade and beer in a blender. Add the lemon juice and lime juice and fill with ice. Process until smooth. Add the sugar, if desired. Pour into glasses.

BERRY SANGRIA

SERVES 12

1 (750-milliliter) bottle syrah or shiraz
1 cup Cognac or brandy
1¹/2 cups orange juice
2 cups lemon-lime sparkling water
3 cups strawberry soda
1 pound fresh strawberries, cut into halves or quarters
1 pint fresh raspberries
1 pint fresh blueberries
¹/2 cup simple syrup (optional)

Stir the wine and Cognac gently in a pitcher. Add the orange juice, sparkling water, soda, strawberries, raspberries and blueberries; mix well. Taste the mixture and add simple syrup 2 tablespoons at a time to sweeten as desired. Serve over ice in glasses.

CHEF'S TIP: If fresh berries are not in season, substitute one 8-ounce package of frozen mixed berries.

Simple Syrup

To make a simple syrup, combine 2 parts sugar and 1 part water in a saucepan. Heat over low heat until the sugar is dissolved, stirring constantly. Let simmer for 5 minutes. Remove from the heat and let stand until cool. Refrigerate until ready to use.

THIS PAGE GRACIOUSLY SPONSORED BY KENNETH AGUILAR & KENDI AGUILAR

Irish Coffee

Courtesy of The Buena Vista

SERVES 1

2 sugar cubes
1/2 cup hot black coffee
1 jigger (1 1/4 ounces) Irish whiskey
Heavy cream, lightly whipped

Fill a 6-ounce, short-stemmed, tulip-shaped coffee glass with very hot water and let stand for 1 or 2 minutes to heat; pour out the water. Place the sugar cubes in the glass and immediately fill 3/4 full with the hot coffee, stirring to dissolve the sugar. Stir in the Irish whiskey. Top with the whipped cream, pouring it over a spoon to form an even head. Serve piping hot.

Hot Spiced Wine

SERVES 8

Peel from 1 orange, cut into strips
1 (8-inch) cinnamon stick, lightly crushed
6 whole cloves
2 cardamom pods, crushed
1 (750-milliliter) bottle dry red wine
1/2 cup raisins
1/3 cup sugar
1/4 cup blanched almonds

Special Equipment: *cheesecloth, kitchen twine*

Prepare two 6- or 8-inch squares of cheesecloth for the spice bag. Layer the cheesecloths and place the orange peel, cinnamon, cloves and cardamom in the center. Bring up the corners of the cheesecloth to enclose the spices and secure with kitchen twine.

Combine the spice bag with the wine, raisins and sugar in a large saucepan. Bring just to a simmer over medium heat and simmer for 10 minutes; do not allow to boil. Remove and discard the spice bag. Stir in the almonds just before serving.

Japanese Ginger au Lait

SERVES 2

¹/2 cup boiling water
1 (2-inch) piece fresh ginger, peeled and thinly sliced
2 shots espresso
1 tablespoon simple syrup or sugar
¹/2 cup steamed milk

Special Equipment: *milk frother*

Pour the boiling water over the ginger in a large heat-resistant glass. Steep for 5 minutes or longer; longer steeping increases the strength of the tea. Strain the tea into two coffee cups. Stir 1 shot of espresso into each cup.

Combine the simple syrup with the milk and froth with a milk frother until warm. Pour into the cups and serve warm.

Chai Tea Latte

A perfect drink for a chilly summer night in San Francisco.

SERVES 2 TO 4

5 black peppercorns
5 green cardamom pods
2 cups water
1 (1-inch) piece fresh ginger, peeled and cut into
    3 or 4 pieces
1 cinnamon stick
¹/2 cup loose-leaf Ceylon tea, or 3 black tea bags
1 cup milk
3 tablespoons sugar, or to taste

Special Equipment: *mortar and pestle, French press*

Crush the peppercorns and cardamom in a mortar with a pestle to release their flavors. Combine with the water, ginger and cinnamon in a 1-quart stainless steel saucepan. Bring to a boil; cover and remove from the heat. Let stand for 5 minutes. Add the tea and steep for 5 minutes longer. Stir in the milk. Heat over low heat for 5 minutes. Remove from the heat and stir in the sugar until dissolved. Pour into a French press, strain and serve hot.

CHEF'S TIP: If you do not have a French press, you can use a coffee filter to strain the tea. If you do not have a mortar and pestle, place the peppercorns and cardamom in a small plastic bag and crush them with the bottom of a saucepan.

Appetizers

In its second decade, the JLSF continued to expand community outreach. In 1923, we founded the Junior League House as temporary housing for children awaiting foster care placement. After years of intensive fund-raising, building planning, and a land purchase, our members opened Pinehaven in 1929 as a larger home to replace the original Junior League House. Meanwhile, in 1926, our distinctive Fashion Show began at monthly meetings over tea. In the same year, we cut the ribbon on a retail store in Tillman Place and opened our business office in the Mark Hopkins Hotel.

Established in 1926, the opulent Mark Hopkins Hotel and its banquet rooms served the most fashionable cuisine of the day. San Francisco appetizers have traditionally included seafood, highlighting the city's proximity to the Pacific Ocean. Mrs. Belle de Graf, a prominent *San Francisco Chronicle* columnist of the time, recommended fish cocktails, raw oysters or clams, canapés of sardines, and lobster or crab as appetizers for home entertaining. Keeping the seafood tradition alive later in the century, the owner of local restaurant Trader Vic's has been credited with masterminding the tasty Crab Rangoon appetizer, wrapping crab meat and cream cheese in a wonton before deep-frying. Additionally, San Francisco's obsession with fresh fruits and vegetables can be found in 1920s' newspaper recipes for appetizers like Grapefruit or Melon Cocktails and Celery with Roquefort Cheese.

As for city landmarks, in 1922 Lombard Street earned its "most crooked street in America" designation when eight switchbacks were designed to help manage car and foot traffic along its steep incline. The Legion of Honor was completed in 1924, a building commissioned as a tribute to California soldiers who died in World War I. In 1927, citizens approved a plan to build the first city-owned opera house in the country. The War Memorial Opera House's Beaux-Arts design would match that of City Hall, the Main Library, and the Legion of Honor.

1921–1930

GINGER CRAB ROLLS

PAIRS WELL WITH ROSATI FAMILY WINERY
CABERNET SAUVIGNON, MENDOCINO COUNTY

MAKES 6 ROLLS

3/4 cup chopped Napa cabbage
1 carrot, chopped
1 tablespoon low-sodium soy sauce
1 tablespoon sesame oil
3/4 teaspoon rice wine vinegar
3/4 teaspoon dry mustard
1/2 teaspoon grated fresh ginger
1/2 teaspoon white pepper
1/4 teaspoon red pepper flakes
1/3 cup fresh Dungeness crab meat, cleaned,
    cooked and chopped
6 square egg roll wrappers
4 cups peanut oil

Combine the cabbage, carrot, soy sauce, sesame oil, rice wine vinegar, dry mustard, ginger, white pepper and red pepper flakes in a bowl and mix well. Fold in the crab meat.

Place one egg roll wrapper at a time on a work surface with one corner at the bottom. Place 1 1/2 tablespoons of the crab meat mixture in the center and fold the bottom corner up over the filling, tucking it under slightly. Moisten the remaining corners and fold the right over the left in the center. Roll the egg roll from the bottom, moistening to seal. Repeat with the remaining wrappers and filling.

Heat the peanut oil to 440 degrees in a medium stockpot over medium-high heat, or until boiling. Add the egg rolls in batches and fry for 3 minutes or until golden brown, turning with tongs, if necessary, to brown evenly. Serve with spicy Chinese mustard and sweet-and-sour sauce.

Smoked Salmon Won Tons with Wasabi Sauce

PAIRS WELL WITH RIESLING

MAKES 12 WON TONS

1/4 cup mayonnaise
1 1/4 teaspoons soy sauce
1 teaspoon lemon juice
1/2 teaspoon wasabi paste
6 (3-inch) square won ton wrappers
1 cup canola oil
4 ounces smoked salmon
12 slices pickled ginger
Chopped chives or daikon sprouts

Whisk the mayonnaise with the soy sauce, lemon juice and wasabi paste in a small bowl for the wasabi sauce.

Cut the won ton wrappers into halves horizontally. Heat the canola oil in a large saucepan. Add the won ton wrappers and fry until golden brown; drain on paper towels.

Place 1/8 teaspoon of the wasabi sauce on each fried won ton. Cut the salmon into twelve slices to fit the won tons and add one slice to each won ton. Spread 1/8 teaspoon of the wasabi sauce over the salmon and top each with a slice of pickled ginger. Sprinkle with chives.

Oyster Mignonette

Courtesy of Swan Oyster Depot

PAIRS WELL WITH HONIG SAUVIGNON BLANC

SERVES 6 TO 8

1 cup rice wine vinegar
1/2 cup finely chopped red onion
1/4 cup finely chopped cilantro
1/4 cup finely chopped jalapeño chiles (optional)
Freshly ground pepper to taste
3 dozen Miyagi or Kumamoto oysters on the half shell

Mix the rice wine vinegar, red onion, cilantro, jalapeño chiles and pepper in a serving bowl for the sauce. Chill until serving time.

Place the oysters in their half shells on a serving platter layered with crushed ice. Serve with the sauce.

THIS PAGE GRACIOUSLY SPONSORED BY ROBYN & RON PAWLO

BUCKWHEAT BLINI WITH OSETRA CAVIAR

Courtesy of Chef Gary Danko of Restaurant Gary Danko

PAIRS WELL WITH GLORIA FERRER CARNEROS CUVÉE

MAKES 50 BLINI

1 cup all-purpose flour
1 tablespoon sugar
1 tablespoon dry yeast
1³/4 cups milk, warmed to 98 degrees
1 cup buckwheat flour
2 teaspoons kosher salt
2 egg yolks
2 egg whites
1/4 cup heavy cream
Clarified butter or vegetable oil
Crème fraîche
Osetra caviar

Stir the all-purpose flour, sugar and yeast together in a bowl. Whisk in 1 cup of the warm milk. Cover with plastic wrap and let stand for 1 hour or until bubbly.

Combine the buckwheat flour and kosher salt in a bowl. Blend the egg yolks with the remaining ³/4 cup warm milk in a small bowl. Whisk into the buckwheat flour mixture. Cover with plastic wrap and let stand for 1 hour. Add to the yeast mixture and mix gently.

Whisk the egg whites in a bowl until soft peaks form. Fold into the yeast mixture. Beat the cream in a bowl until soft peaks form. Fold into the yeast mixture. Let stand at room temperature for 1 hour or longer.

Heat a nonstick pan over medium heat. Spread a thin layer of clarified butter over the bottom and heat until hot. Add 1 tablespoon of the batter at a time to the pan and cook until the edge is golden brown. Turn and cook until golden brown on the bottom. Remove to a paper towel. Repeat with the remaining batter, adding butter as needed. Serve hot with a dollop of crème fraîche and top with caviar.

CHEF'S TIP: If you have leftover batter, use it to make delicious breakfast pancakes.

Caviar

The three prominent types of caviar are beluga, osetra, and sevruga. Beluga is prized for its light gray to jet-black color, size, and delicate flavor. The dark green to pale amber osetra is known for its subtle flavor. Sevruga is the least expensive of the three, and while the color is similar to beluga, it is known as the saltiest. Always serve caviar with a spoon made of mother-of-pearl, bone, or glass.

Tuna Tartare

PAIRS WELL WITH GLORIA FERRER SONOMA BRUT

SERVES 8

3 tablespoons extra-virgin olive oil
3 tablespoons lime juice
2 tablespoons soy sauce
4 dashes of hot sauce
Grated zest of 1 lime
1 teaspoon salt
1 teaspoon freshly ground pepper
12 ounces sashimi-grade tuna steak
1/3 cup minced green onions
1 avocado, cut into small pieces

Blend the olive oil, lime juice, soy sauce, hot sauce, lime zest, salt and pepper in a large bowl. Cut the tuna into 1/4-inch pieces. Add to the olive oil mixture. Stir in the green onions and avocado.

Marinate in the refrigerator for 45 minutes or longer. Serve with crispy won ton strips (see page 32) or rice crackers.

Red Snapper Ceviche with Green Apple

Ceviche is made by "cooking" the fish using the acid of the citrus fruits.

PAIRS WELL WITH GLORIA FERRER ROYAL CUVÉE

SERVES 4

1 pound fresh red snapper, deboned and
    cut into 1/2-inch chunks
Juice of 1 1/2 lemons
1/2 teaspoon salt
1/4 teaspoon freshly ground pepper
1 Granny Smith apple, peeled and cut into 1-inch pieces
1 jalapeño chile, seeded and finely chopped
1/2 red onion, thinly sliced
1 tablespoon chopped fresh cilantro

Combine the red snapper with the lemon juice, salt and pepper in a small shallow dish; mix to coat the fish evenly. Top with the apple, jalapeño chile, onion and cilantro. Marinate in the refrigerator for 1 hour; stir to mix well. Marinate for 2 hours longer or until the fish is opaque and white. Stir and spoon into martini glasses to serve.

This page graciously sponsored by Lillian Phan

PROSCIUTTO AND SAGE PINWHEELS

MAKES 80 TO 100 PINWHEELS

2 sheets puff pastry
1 egg, lightly beaten
8 slices prosciutto
3/4 cup (3 ounces) shredded mozzarella cheese
1/4 cup (1 ounce) grated Parmesan cheese
1/4 cup chopped fresh sage
Freshly cracked pepper to taste

Place the puff pastry sheets on lightly floured waxed paper with the narrow end at the bottom. Roll gently to remove the ridges. Cut each sheet in half crosswise to make four 6×12-inch sheets. Brush the long top edge of each sheet with the egg. Overlap two pieces of prosciutto on each sheet, leaving the portion brushed with egg uncovered.

Mix the mozzarella cheese, Parmesan cheese and sage in a bowl. Spread evenly over the prosciutto and sprinkle with pepper. Roll each pastry from the bottom to enclose the filling; press to seal. Wrap in waxed paper and freeze seam side down for 3 hours or longer.

Preheat the oven to 400 degrees. Remove the waxed paper from two of the rolls and cut the rolls into 1/2-inch slices. Arrange the slices cut side down 1 inch apart on a baking sheet lined with baking parchment. Bake for 15 minutes or until puffed and golden brown. Cool on a wire rack for 2 minutes and serve warm. Repeat the procedure with the remaining rolls.

CHEF'S TIP: You can bake the number of pinwheels needed, leaving the remaining logs in the freezer for up to three days.

SPICED BEEF PHYLLO CUPS WITH MINT AND FETA

MAKES 24 CUPS

24 miniature phyllo cups
1 tablespoon olive oil
1/2 cup chopped onion
1 tablespoon minced garlic
4 ounces ground beef or ground lamb
1/4 cup dried currants
3/4 teaspoon ground cumin
1/2 teaspoon each ground ginger and ground cinnamon
1/8 teaspoon ground allspice
1/4 teaspoon sea salt
1/8 teaspoon freshly ground pepper
2 tablespoons julienned mint
2 tablespoons crumbled feta cheese

Preheat the oven to 350 degrees. Arrange the phyllo cups on a baking sheet and bake for 3 to 5 minutes or until heated through. Heat the olive oil in a sauté pan and add the onion and garlic. Sauté until the onion is tender. Add the ground beef, currants, cumin, ginger, cinnamon, allspice, sea salt and pepper. Sauté for 5 minutes or until the ground beef is brown and crumbly. Stir in the mint. Spoon 1 heaping teaspoonful of the beef mixture into each cup. Top with the feta cheese and serve warm.

Fresh Herbs or DRIED HERBS

It's easy to exchange fresh herbs and dried herbs in a recipe. Just remember that it takes twice the amount of fresh herbs as dried herbs called for, or half the amount of dried herbs as fresh herbs.

PESTO AND GOAT CHEESE TARTS

MAKES 24 TARTS

Pesto
3 cups tightly packed fresh basil leaves
1/2 cup toasted pine nuts
2 garlic cloves
1 teaspoon salt, or more to taste
1/2 teaspoon freshly ground pepper, or more to taste
1 cup (or more) extra-virgin olive oil
3/4 cup (3 ounces) grated Parmesan cheese

Goat Cheese Tarts
1 (2-crust) package refrigerator pie pastry,
    at room temperature
16 ounces goat cheese or chèvre, crumbled
1 (6- to 8-ounce) jar sun-dried tomatoes, drained

Pesto
Place the basil, pine nuts, garlic, salt and pepper in a food processor and pulse until finely chopped. Add the olive oil gradually, processing constantly until smooth, adding additional oil if needed to reach the desired consistency. Add the cheese and pulse just until blended.

Tarts
Preheat the oven to 350 degrees. Remove one pastry at a time and roll on a lightly floured work surface until slightly thinner. Cut the pastry into 3-inch circles. Press the circles into miniature muffin cups, lining the walls evenly. Spoon pesto into each cup, filling halfway. Spoon the goat cheese over the pesto and top each with a sun-dried tomato.

Bake the tarts for 15 minutes or until the cheese is bubbly and the pastry is light golden brown. Serve hot.

CHEF'S TIP: Substitute 16 ounces of packaged fresh pesto for the homemade pesto to prepare the tarts in a hurry.

CRANBERRY BRIE

PAIRS WELL WITH GLORIA FERRER SONOMA BRUT

SERVES 6 TO 8

1 pound fresh cranberries
1 (9-ounce) jar orange marmalade
1/2 cup dried currants
1 1/2 cups packed brown sugar
2 tablespoons brandy
1 teaspoon cinnamon
1/2 teaspoon ground cloves
1 cup walnuts, chopped
1 (18-ounce) round Brie cheese, at room temperature

Combine the cranberries, marmalade, currants, brown sugar, brandy, cinnamon and cloves in a heavy saucepan. Simmer for 15 to 20 minutes or until the cranberries pop. Remove from the heat and stir in the walnuts.

Place the Brie on a serving plate. Spoon the cranberry mixture over the top. Serve with baguette slices, water crackers and/or sliced green apples.

CHEF'S TIP: This dish can be prepared in advance and frozen. Simply reheat the Brie in the oven to serve.

Mushroom Pâté with Pickled Red Onion Confit

PAIRS WELL WITH FAR NIENTE ESTATE BOTTLED CHARDONNAY

SERVES 6 TO 8

Red Onion Confit
1/4 cup red wine vinegar
3 tablespoons sugar
2 garlic cloves
Pinch of mustard seeds
Pinch of red pepper flakes
1 large red onion, thinly sliced

Mushroom Pâté
1 cup (2 sticks) butter
1 pound mixed portobello, shiitake and brown button
    mushroom caps, chopped
1/2 onion, chopped
2 garlic cloves, chopped
1 small French roll, torn into small pieces
8 ounces cream cheese, softened
2 tablespoons chopped parsley
Salt and freshly ground pepper to taste

Croutes and Assembly
1 (18-inch) sourdough baguette
1 cup olive oil
Salt to taste

Confit
Mix the rice wine vinegar with the sugar, garlic, mustard seeds and red pepper flakes in a saucepan. Bring to a boil. Add the onion and cook until the onion is tender and pink. Cool to room temperature and remove the garlic.

Pâté
Melt the butter in a heavy skillet. Add the mushrooms, onion and garlic. Sweat until the vegetables are tender. Add the bread and mix well. Cool to room temperature. Combine with the cream cheese and parsley in a blender or food processor and process until smooth. Season with salt and pepper.

Croutes and Assembly
Preheat the oven to 350 degrees. Cut the baguette into thin slices. Toss with the olive oil and salt in a bowl, coating evenly. Arrange on a baking sheet and bake for 8 to 10 minutes or until crisp, turning halfway through the cooking time.

To serve, spread the pâté on the toasted baguette slices and top with the confit.

Mingle the Guests

Place appetizers and hors d'oeuvres throughout the house to encourage guests to mingle.

CALIFORNIA CAVIAR

SERVES 4 TO 6

California Caviar Dressing
1/4 cup extra-virgin olive oil
1/4 cup red wine vinegar
Juice of 1/2 lime
2 garlic cloves, crushed
1 teaspoon ground cumin
3/4 teaspoon salt
Pinch of freshly ground pepper

California Caviar
1 1/3 cups dried black-eyed peas, cooked and drained, or
    2 (15-ounce) cans black-eyed peas, drained
1 (15-ounce) can white corn, drained
3 avocados, chopped
2 cups chopped seeded fresh tomatoes
1 bunch cilantro, chopped
3/4 cup chopped green onions
1 jalapeño chile, seeded and chopped

Dressing
Whisk the olive oil, red wine vinegar, lime juice and garlic in a bowl. Add the cumin, salt and pepper; whisk until combined.

Caviar
Mix the black-eyed peas, corn, avocados, tomatoes, cilantro, green onions and jalapeño chile in a large bowl. Add the dressing and mix gently. Chill for 1 hour. Serve with tortilla chips.

WHITE BEAN DIP WITH TOASTED PITA

SERVES 6 TO 8

Toasted Pita
1 package white or whole wheat pita rounds
Extra-virgin olive oil
1 to 2 teaspoons freshly ground coriander
Sea salt and freshly ground pepper to taste

White Bean Dip
2 (15-ounce) cans cannelloni beans, drained and rinsed
1 garlic clove, crushed
1/4 cup extra-virgin olive oil
Juice of 1 lemon
1 teaspoon dried dill weed
1/2 teaspoon each dried rosemary, thyme and parsley
2 teaspoons sea salt
1/2 teaspoon freshly ground pepper
Parsley or cilantro, for garnish

Pita
Preheat the oven to 350 degrees. Brush both sides of the pita rounds with olive oil and sprinkle lightly with coriander, sea salt and pepper. Cut each pita round into eight triangles and arrange on a baking sheet. Bake on the center oven rack for 15 minutes or until light brown. Cool to room temperature on the baking sheet.

Dip
Combine the beans, garlic, olive oil, lemon juice, dill weed, rosemary, thyme, parsley, sea salt and pepper in a food processor. Process for 2 minutes or until smooth, scraping down the side of the food processor occasionally. Chill in the refrigerator for 30 minutes. Adjust the lemon juice and sea salt as needed. Spoon into a serving bowl and garnish with a sprig of parsley; serve with the toasted pita.

WINE COUNTRY GUACAMOLE

SERVES 4 TO 6

2 small red onions, chopped
3 tablespoons chopped garlic
1/4 cup red wine
2 tablespoons olive oil
1 tablespoon balsamic vinegar
4 avocados
1 1/2 teaspoons fresh lemon juice
2 tablespoons chopped cilantro
1 jalapeño chile, seeded and chopped
Salt and freshly ground pepper to taste

Preheat the oven to 425 degrees. Mix the onions, garlic, red wine, olive oil and balsamic vinegar in a small bowl. Spread on a foil-lined baking sheet and bake for 30 minutes, stirring after 15 minutes. Cool to room temperature.

Mash the avocados in a medium bowl. Add the roasted onion mixture, lemon juice, cilantro and jalapeño chile and mix well. Season with salt and pepper. Chill in the refrigerator for 1 hour. Serve with tortilla chips.

CHEF'S TIP: To keep guacamole from turning brown, press plastic wrap directly on the surface of the guacamole to keep the air out. Refrigerate until ready to serve.

FIG AND BLUE CHEESE POPPERS

PAIRS WELL WITH DOLCE, CALIFORNIA
LATE HARVEST WINE

SERVES 10 TO 12

12 to 15 fresh black Mission figs (about 1 to 1 1/2 pounds)
4 to 6 ounces Point Reyes blue cheese
Honey

Preheat the broiler. Remove the stems from the figs gently to keep the top point of each fig intact. Cut each fig into halves through the tip to create two teardrop-shaped halves. Cut the blue cheese into 1/2-inch cubes. Press one cube gently into the soft center of each fig. Arrange the figs, cheese side up, on a baking sheet. Broil for 1 to 2 minutes or just until the cheese is softened. Arrange in a circle on a round plate and drizzle lightly with honey. You can use crumbly blue cheese, if desired.

Avocados

Avocados can be found year-round in San Francisco, with their peak from March to May. Hass avocadoes are dark green to almost black with a pebbled skin. They have a buttery flavor, preferred for use in guacamole.

DRIED APRICOTS WITH GORGONZOLA, GOAT CHEESE AND TOASTED PISTACHIOS

MAKES 20 APPETIZERS

20 dried apricots
1/2 cup fresh orange juice
1/4 cup finely crushed pistachios
2 ounces Gorgonzola cheese or Cambozola cheese,
   at room temperature
3 ounces goat cheese, at room temperature

Combine the apricots with the orange juice in a glass dish and let stand for 20 minutes or until soft and plump. Drain and pat dry with paper towels.

Toast the pistachios in a sauté pan, shaking until the nuts are pale golden brown and fragrant. Combine the Gorgonzola cheese and goat cheese in a mixing bowl and beat until smooth and creamy.

Spoon the cheese mixture into a pastry bag and pipe 1/2 teaspoon onto each apricot. Top each with 1/4 teaspoon toasted pistachios. You can also spoon the cheese mixture onto the apricots if you prefer.

ROSEMARY-BROWN SUGAR CASHEWS

MAKES 4 CUPS

4 cups raw cashews
1 egg white
1/3 cup packed brown sugar
Leaves of 2 sprigs of fresh rosemary
1 tablespoon vegetable oil
1 teaspoon salt
1/2 teaspoon pepper

Preheat the oven to 325 degrees. Spread the cashews on a baking parchment-lined baking sheet. Toast for 5 to 10 minutes or until light golden and fragrant, stirring frequently to ensure even browning. Cool for 15 minutes.

Whisk the egg white in a large bowl until foamy. Add the brown sugar, rosemary, oil, salt and pepper and mix well. Stir in the cashews, coating evenly. Spread on the baking sheet and toast for 5 minutes longer or until the cashews are golden brown and the brown sugar has crystallized. Cool and serve.

CHEF'S TIP: These can be prepared several days in advance and stored in an airtight container to retain their maximum freshness.

Salads and Soups

In 1935, the Association of Junior Leagues International (AJLI) held its 15th Annual Conference in San Francisco. The conference remains historic in articulating an enduring philosophy of service: Leagues could be most useful by meeting community needs in a variety of areas instead of providing permanent support to any one project. It was recommended that after a project demonstrated success it should be turned over to an appropriate community agency, thus enabling Leagues to move on to other projects that needed their assistance. The JLSF kicked off the decade by staging *Snow White and the Seven Dwarfs*. The play would be the first of many bi-annual productions by the JLSF for the San Francisco Children's Theater Association.

A theatre production may have inspired San Francisco's famous Green Goddess Dressing. Rumor has it that Chef Philip Roemer of the Palace Hotel developed the mayonnaise, tarragon, and chive dressing at the request of actor George Arliss, who starred in San Francisco's production of a play called *The Green Goddess*. Originally created in the 1920s, by the end of the 1930s Roemer's recipe had become famous, circulating throughout cookbook, newspaper, and magazine recipes.

The War Memorial Opera House and Veterans Building were completed in 1932. The Opera House provided a beautiful home to the San Francisco Opera Ballet, which was founded in 1933. Coit Tower, designed to resemble a firehose nozzle, was completed in 1933 and dedicated to firefighters who served in the 1906 earthquake. The middle years of the decade saw the completion of San Francisco's landmark bridges, allowing the San Francisco Bay to be crossed by car and foot traffic. Previously, ferries managed all cross-bay travel. The Bay Bridge opened in 1936, with the Golden Gate Bridge following in 1937. The Golden Gate International Exposition celebrated completion of the two bridges on the manmade Treasure Island festival site.

1931–1940

Green Goddess Salad Dressing

Recipe from San Francisco á la Carte *cookbook.*

MAKES 2 CUPS

1³/4 cups mayonnaise
1/4 cup sour cream
1/4 cup tarragon vinegar
6 to 8 anchovy fillets, mashed, or
  3 to 4 teaspoons anchovy paste
1 garlic clove, minced
3 tablespoons minced fresh tarragon leaves
2 tablespoons minced fresh chives
1 tablespoon chopped fresh parsley

Blend the mayonnaise, sour cream and tarragon vinegar in a jar. Add the anchovies, garlic, tarragon, chives and parsley; shake or stir to mix well. Let stand for 1 hour or longer to blend the flavors. Store in the refrigerator for several days.

Green Goddess Salad

Since the dressing was created, Green Goddess Salad became a permanent menu item at the historic Palace Hotel. Today the salad is referred to as The Garden Court Crab Salad and features farm-fresh mixed baby greens, locally grown California vegetables, and a generous portion of Dungeness crab meat.

CALIFORNIA GODDESS DIP AND DRESSING

A California twist on a San Francisco classic.

MAKES 1¹/2 CUPS

1 cup chopped avocado (about 1 avocado)
3 or 4 anchovy fillets, mashed, or 1¹/2 to 2 teaspoons
*   anchovy paste*
2 garlic cloves, minced
2 scallions, chopped
¹/4 cup fresh basil, chopped
1 tablespoon chopped fresh parsley
1 tablespoon minced fresh tarragon leaves
¹/4 cup sour cream or Greek yogurt
¹/4 cup white wine vinegar
1¹/2 tablespoons lemon juice
Extra-virgin olive oil (optional)

Combine the avocado, anchovies, garlic, scallions, basil, parsley and tarragon in a food processor. Add the sour cream, white wine vinegar and lemon juice. Process until smooth. Serve with crudités as a dip or over steamed green vegetables.

For dressing, add olive oil ¹/4 cup at a time, processing constantly until the desired consistency is reached. Toss with salad greens.

MEXICAN VINAIGRETTE

MAKES 1¹/4 CUPS

2/3 cup canola oil
¹/2 cup fresh lemon juice
¹/2 cup fresh lime juice
3 tablespoons honey
2 tablespoons chopped fresh cilantro leaves
1 garlic clove, minced
1 teaspoon minced seeded jalapeño chile
1 teaspoon ground cumin
Salt and freshly ground pepper to taste

Whisk the canola oil, lemon juice, lime juice and honey in a bowl. Add the cilantro, garlic, jalapeño chile and cumin; whisk until combined. Season with salt and pepper. Serve tossed with a salad of mixed greens, black beans, jicama, roasted red pepper, corn and shredded cheese.

CHEF'S TIP: Marinate chicken or seafood in Mexican Vinaigrette for several hours before grilling.

GRILLED PEACHES WITH WARM PANCETTA AND FRISÉE SALAD

Courtesy of Chef Mark Gordon, Rose's Café

SERVES 4

2 ripe peaches, each cut into 8 slices
Olive oil for brushing
Salt and pepper to taste
1/4 cup chopped pancetta lardons
1/4 cup extra-virgin olive oil
2 tablespoons lemon juice
1 tablespoon Dijon mustard
1/4 teaspoon ground star anise
6 cups tender yellow and white frisée leaves

Brush the peaches with olive oil and season with salt and pepper. Grill until light brown and heated through; keep warm.

Sauté the pancetta in a sauté pan over low heat until light brown; drain. Add 1/4 cup olive oil, the lemon juice, Dijon mustard and star anise and mix well. Add the frisée and toss over low heat just until warm.

Spoon the frisée onto serving plates and top with the peaches. Drizzle with additional olive oil.

ARUGULA SALAD WITH MUSHROOMS, FENNEL AND SHAVED PARMESAN

Courtesy of Chef Pablo Estrada, Rose Pistola

SERVES 4

Lemon Vinaigrette
2 tablespoons lemon juice
1/4 cup grated lemon zest
1 tablespoon Champagne vinegar
1 tablespoon minced shallot
3/4 cup extra-virgin olive oil
3/4 cup pure olive oil

Salad
2 cups sliced cremini mushrooms
4 teaspoons white truffle oil
2 cups shaved fennel bulbs
2 cups torn large arugula leaves
2 ounces (1/2 cup) shaved Grana Padano or
    Parmesan cheese

Vinaigrette
Whisk the lemon juice, lemon zest, Champagne vinegar and shallots together in a bowl. Whisk in both olive oils. Let stand at room temperature until serving time. The vinaigrette can stand at room temperature for up to 1 day; place any unused vinaigrette in the refrigerator for longer storage.

Salad
Toss the mushrooms with the truffle oil in a bowl. Add the fennel and arugula. Drizzle with the desired amount of the vinaigrette and toss to coat evenly. Spoon onto salad plates and top with the cheese.

Pomegranate Salad with Pomegranate Raspberry Vinaigrette

Pomegranates are in season during the fall and winter months and add beautiful color to any meal.

PAIRS WELL WITH HONIG SAUVIGNON BLANC

SERVES 6

Pomegranate Raspberry Vinaigrette

1 small shallot
1/4 cup raspberry vinegar
1/4 cup pomegranate juice
1 1/2 cups extra-virgin olive oil
Salt and freshly ground pepper to taste

Pomegranate Salad

1/2 head romaine
1/2 head red leaf lettuce
1 Granny Smith apple, coarsely chopped
1 small red bell pepper, finely chopped
1/4 cup dried cranberries
1/2 cup hazelnuts, toasted and chopped
4 ounces crumbled blue cheese
1/2 to 1 cup fresh pomegranate seeds

Vinaigrette

Combine the shallot, raspberry vinegar and pomegranate juice in a blender or food processor. Pulse until the shallot is finely chopped. Add the olive oil gradually, processing constantly until smooth. Season with salt and pepper. Store in the refrigerator.

Salad

Cut the half heads of romaine and red leaf lettuce lengthwise into halves, cutting to but not through the cores. Cut crosswise into 3/4-inch slices, discarding the cores. Combine with the apple, bell pepper and dried cranberries in a bowl. Add the desired amount of vinaigrette and toss to coat evenly. Spoon onto a serving platter and top with the hazelnuts, cheese and pomegranate seeds.

Toasted Hazelnuts

Spread the hazelnuts in a single layer on a baking sheet. Toast at 350 degrees on the center oven rack for 10 to 15 minutes or until the skins are blistered and the hazelnuts are light brown, watching carefully to prevent burning. Wrap in a cotton kitchen towel and steam for 1 minute. Rub the hazelnuts in the towel to remove the loose skins and cool to room temperature.

BAKED GOAT CHEESE SALAD

PAIRS WELL WITH A HARD APPLE CIDER OR
PEAR CIDER

Goat Cheese Medallions

2 (8-ounce) logs soft goat cheese

1 cup panko (Japanese bread crumbs)

1 sprig of fresh thyme or parsley, chopped

1/4 teaspoon each salt and freshly ground pepper

1 egg

1 teaspoon water

Salad

1/2 cup extra-virgin olive oil

1/4 cup sherry vinegar

1/2 shallot, chopped

Juice of 1/2 lemon

1/4 teaspoon each salt and pepper

8 cups fresh organic greens

Medallions

Preheat the oven to 350 degrees. Place the goat cheese logs in the freezer and freeze for 20 minutes. Mix the panko with the thyme, salt and pepper in a bowl. Toast on a baking sheet in the oven for 3 to 5 minutes. Maintain the oven temperature. Beat the egg lightly with the water in a small bowl. Cut each cheese log crosswise into six slices. Dip the slices into the egg wash and then into the panko mixture. Arrange the medallions on a baking sheet lined with baking parchment. Bake for 17 to 20 minutes or until golden brown.

Salad

Whisk the olive oil, sherry vinegar, shallot, lemon juice, salt and pepper in a bowl while the medallions are baking. Add the greens to the dressing at serving time. Spoon onto six serving plates and top each with two warm goat cheese medallions. Serve immediately.

INDIAN SPINACH SALAD

SERVES 4 TO 6

Curry Chutney Dressing

1/4 cup vegetable oil, canola oil or safflower oil

1/4 cup white wine vinegar

2 tablespoons mango, peach, pear or apple chutney

2 tablespoons sugar

1 1/2 teaspoons curry powder

1/2 teaspoon salt

Spinach Salad

6 cups baby spinach

1 1/2 cups chopped peeled Fuji apples or Gala apples

1/2 cup raisins

1/2 cup hot and spicy peanuts, coarsely chopped

2 tablespoons sliced green onions

Dressing

Combine the oil, white wine vinegar, chutney, sugar, curry powder and salt in a small bowl; whisk until well mixed.

Salad

Combine the spinach, apples, raisins, peanuts and green onions in a salad bowl. Add the dressing at serving time and toss to coat evenly.

BEET AND FRENCH LENTIL SALAD WITH LEMON

SERVES 8 TO 10

Lemon Vinaigrette

Juice of 2 lemons
1 teaspoon grated
    lemon zest
1/4 cup extra-virgin olive oil
1 shallot, finely chopped
Salt to taste

Roasted Beets

6 red beets, trimmed
1 1/2 tablespoons olive oil
2 tablespoons balsamic
    vinegar
6 sprigs of fresh marjoram
Salt and freshly ground
    pepper to taste

French Lentils

10 sprigs of fresh parsley,
    chopped
10 peppercorns, cracked
5 sprigs of thyme
2 garlic cloves, crushed
2 bay leaves
1 1/2 tablespoons olive oil
1 small yellow onion,
    finely chopped
16 ounces French green
    lentils, rinsed and sorted
2 carrots, cut into thirds
2 teaspoons salt

Assembly

2 tablespoons sherry vinegar,
    balsamic vinegar or red
    wine vinegar
1/2 cup chopped fresh
    parsley
3 tablespoons chopped
    fresh mint leaves
8 ounces (2 cups) crumbled
    feta cheese
Grated lemon zest, parsley
    and mint, for garnish

Special Equipment:
    cheesecloth,
    kitchen twine

Vinaigrette

Whisk three quarters of the lemon juice, the lemon zest, olive oil, shallot and salt together in a bowl. Reserve the remaining lemon juice for another use or discard.

Beets

Preheat the oven to 400 degrees. Place the beets on a large sheet of foil. Sprinkle with the olive oil, balsamic vinegar and marjoram. Season with salt and pepper. Fold the foil to enclose the beets and place in a roasting pan or baking dish. Roast for 1 hour or until tender but still firm. Cool to room temperature. Peel the beets and cut into medium cubes.

Lentils

Place the parsley, peppercorns, thyme, garlic and bay leaves on a square of cheesecloth. Tie the cheesecloth into a bag to enclose the seasonings and tie with kitchen twine for a bouquet garni.

Heat the olive oil in a large saucepan or Dutch oven over medium heat. Add the onion and sweat for 10 minutes or until translucent. Add the lentils, carrots, bouquet garni, salt and 5 cups water. Bring to a boil and simmer for 25 to 30 minutes or until the lentils are tender. Remove and discard the bouquet garni and carrots. Strain the lentils to remove all liquid.

Assembly

Spoon the lentils into a large serving bowl. Add the beets, sherry vinegar and lemon vinaigrette to the warm lentils and let stand for 10 minutes to blend the flavors. Spoon onto serving plates and sprinkle with the parsley and mint. Top with the cheese at serving time to prevent discoloration from the beets. Garnish with grated lemon zest, parsley and mint.

Summer Corn Salad

PAIRS WELL WITH DRY ROSÉ

SERVES 6

Lime Dressing
Juice of 3 limes
2 jalapeño chiles, seeded and finely chopped
1 teaspoon ground cumin
1/4 cup olive oil

Corn Salad
5 ears corn
3 bunches scallions, trimmed to white and
*   light green portions*
Olive oil
Salt and freshly ground pepper to taste
2 cups grape tomatoes, cut into halves
3/4 cup chopped cilantro
1 1/4 cups crumbled feta cheese

Dressing
Mix the lime juice with the jalapeño chiles and cumin in a small bowl. Whisk in the olive oil until combined.

Salad
Brush the corn and scallions with olive oil and season generously with salt and pepper. Grill the corn over medium-high heat for 10 to 15 minutes or until tender, turning frequently. Grill the scallions for 1 to 2 minutes on each side or until tender. Cut the scallions into 1/2-inch pieces.

Cut the kernels from the corn ears into a bowl. Add the scallions, tomatoes and cilantro. Add the desired amount of dressing gradually, stirring to coat well. Store any unused dressing in the refrigerator. Fold in the cheese. Season with salt and pepper.

Drunken Crab Soup

PAIRS WELL WITH INDIA PALE ALE

SERVES 4

1/4 cup (1/2 stick) butter
1 yellow onion, chopped
2 tablespoons all-purpose flour
1 teaspoon paprika
1/2 teaspoon cumin
1/2 teaspoon fennel seeds, crushed
1/2 teaspoon salt
1/4 teaspoon pepper
2 cups water
2 teaspoons crab base
1 cup half-and-half
2 tablespoons sherry
1 cup crab meat

Special Equipment: *sieve*

Melt the butter in a medium stockpot over medium heat and heat until the foam subsides. Add the onion and sauté for 6 minutes or until translucent. Stir in the flour, paprika, cumin, fennel seeds, salt and pepper. Sauté for 1 minute. Add the water and crab base and mix well. Bring to a boil. Cover and reduce the heat to low. Simmer for 1 hour.

Process in a food processor or with an immersion blender until smooth. Pour through a sieve back into the stockpot. Place over low heat and add the half-and-half, sherry and crab meat, mixing gently. Simmer, covered, for 30 minutes or until heated through. Serve warm.

CHEF'S TIP: Crab base can be found in specialty grocery stores or purchased on the internet. You can also substitute 2 cups fish stock for the crab base and water.

Tortilla Soup

SERVES 6 TO 8

Soup
2 tablespoons butter
1/4 cup vegetable oil
6 ribs celery, chopped
4 garlic cloves, chopped
2 large carrots, chopped
1 large yellow onion, chopped
1 jalapeño chile, seeded
  and chopped
Shredded breast meat from
  2 rotisserie chickens
1/2 cup all-purpose flour
1 tablespoon hot sauce
1 tablespoon ground cumin
1 tablespoon chili powder
1 tablespoon salt
1 tablespoon lemon pepper
1 (14-ounce) can
  whole tomatoes
5 1/4 cups chicken broth

Toppings
Tortilla Strips (see below)
1 cup sour cream
1 or 2 avocados, chopped
1 cup (4 ounces) shredded
  Cheddar or Monterey
  Jack cheese
1 cup chopped cilantro

Heat the butter and oil in a large nonstick stockpot over medium-high heat. Add the celery, garlic, carrots, onion and jalapeño chile. Sauté for 5 minutes or until the onion is translucent. Stir in the chicken, flour, hot sauce, cumin, chili powder, salt and lemon pepper. Add the tomatoes, cutting through with a knife to chop. Stir in the broth. Simmer for 1 hour. Serve with the toppings.

Tortilla Strips

Cut 8 corn tortillas into strips. Heat 1 tablespoon vegetable oil in a large skillet over high heat. Fry the strips in batches for 2 to 3 minutes or until light brown, tossing occasionally to brown evenly and adding oil as needed. Drain on paper towels.

SPICY LEEK AND PEANUT SOUP

Serve with roasted chicken and a green salad or with Toasted Pita (see page 40).

SERVES 8

2 tablespoons peanut oil or olive oil
4 garlic cloves, minced
3 ribs celery, chopped
2 large leeks, coarsely chopped
1 red onion, chopped
2 teaspoons curry powder
1 teaspoon ground cumin
1 teaspoon ground coriander
3/4 teaspoon cayenne pepper
3 cups chopped seeded Roma tomatoes
   (about 6 tomatoes)
1 cup salted roasted peanuts
4 cups chicken stock
1 cup chopped seeded Roma tomatoes
   (about 2 tomatoes)
1 cup salted roasted peanuts
2 tablespoons sugar
Sea salt to taste
1/2 cup heavy cream (optional)
1/4 cup chopped chives, for garnish
1/4 cup chopped peanuts, for garnish

Heat the peanut oil in a large stockpot over low heat. Add the garlic, celery, leeks and onion and sauté until tender. Add the curry powder, cumin, coriander and cayenne pepper. Increase the heat to medium-high and cook for 3 to 5 minutes, stirring occasionally. Add 3 cups tomatoes and 1 cup peanuts and cook for 5 minutes longer. Stir in the stock and bring to a boil. Reduce the heat and cover; simmer for 15 minutes.

Combine 1 cup tomatoes, 1 cup peanuts and the sugar in a food processor and process until smooth. You can also use a blender, beginning with the tomatoes and adding the peanuts next and the sugar last. Add to the soup and simmer for 5 minutes longer or until thickened. Season with sea salt. Add the heavy cream and bring just to a boil. Garnish servings with the chives and 1/4 cup chopped peanuts.

Preparing Leeks

After washing the leeks, cut off the green leaves and the root. Slice each leek in half lengthwise. Place the leeks flat side down on a cutting board and slice each lengthwise into 1 1/2- to 2-inch long, 1/8-inch wide strips. Remove the grit by placing the chopped leeks in a bowl of cold water. Swirl around and then leave them undisturbed for a couple minutes. Carefully remove the leeks from the water and pat dry.

POTATO LEEK SOUP

Courtesy of Chef Jennie Lorenzo, Fifth Floor

SERVES 8

Soup

1 pound Yukon Gold potatoes, peeled and cut into quarters
2 cups (4 sticks) plus 2 tablespoons butter
1/3 cup thinly sliced halved shallots
1 cup thinly sliced halved leeks, white and
    light green portions only
6 tablespoons thinly sliced garlic
3 cups chicken stock
3 cups water
1/2 cup heavy cream
Juice of 1/2 lemon
Salt to taste

Toppings

Thinly sliced truffles
Camembert cheese
Celery leaves
Crispy potatoes (see right)

Special Equipment: *mandoline, immersion blender,*
    fine mesh sieve

Cut the potatoes into very thin slices with a mandoline. Melt the butter in a stockpot and add the shallots, leeks and garlic. Sauté over low heat until tender and translucent. Add the potatoes and cook until slightly tender. Add the stock and water and bring to a simmer. Simmer for 25 to 30 minutes or until the potatoes are very tender.

Process the soup at high speed with an immersion blender. Strain through a fine mesh sieve into a saucepan. Add the heavy cream, lemon juice and salt. Cook just until heated through. Serve with the toppings.

Crispy Potatoes

To prepare Crispy Potatoes, cut a Yukon potato into 1/2×3/4×3-inch strips. Thinly slice the strips using a mandoline. Blanch the slices in hot water for 1 minute. Drain and pat dry. Fry the slices in hot oil in a skillet until crispy. Remove to paper towels. Season with salt and let cool.

THIS PAGE GRACIOUSLY SPONSORED BY KIMBERLY & COLIN O'CONNELL

Curried Butternut Squash Soup

Courtesy of Chef Ryan Scott, Ryan Scott 2 Go

SERVES 12

2 1/2 pounds butternut squash, peeled and cut into 1-inch pieces
2 tablespoons extra-virgin olive oil
2 tablespoons unsalted butter
1 yellow onion, chopped
1 shallot, chopped
1 leek, chopped (white and light green portions only)
2 stalks lemongrass, minced
1 ounce fresh ginger, minced
2 garlic cloves, minced
2 tablespoons curry powder
1 teaspoon ground cumin
12 cups vegetable stock
1 cup coconut milk
2 cups heavy cream
1 tablespoon salt
Crème fraîche and chopped pistachios, for garnish

Special Equipment: *immersion blender*

Preheat the oven to 425 degrees. Toss the butternut squash with the olive oil in a bowl and spread on a baking sheet. Roast for 30 minutes or until tender, rotating and stirring halfway through the roasting time. Melt the butter in a large stockpot. Add the onion, shallot, leek, lemongrass, ginger, garlic, curry powder and cumin. Sauté for 10 minutes or until tender. Add the roasted squash, stock, coconut milk, heavy cream and salt. Bring to a boil. Reduce the heat and simmer for 30 minutes. Remove from the heat and purée with an immersion blender or food processor. Garnish servings with crème fraîche and chopped pistachios.

Heirloom Tomato Gazpacho

Fresh ingredients are essential! Heirloom tomatoes are in season from July through September in California. Serve gazpacho in shot glasses for a party appetizer.

PAIRS WELL WITH ROSATI FAMILY WINERY CABERNET SAUVIGNON, MENDOCINO COUNTY

SERVES 8

6 heirloom tomatoes, chopped
1 large cucumber, chopped
1 small white onion, chopped
1 red bell pepper, chopped
8 large basil leaves
2 cups tomato juice
3 tablespoons fresh lemon juice
1/4 cup extra-virgin olive oil
2 tablespoons red wine vinegar
2 tablespoons sour cream
1/2 teaspoon anchovy paste
2 teaspoons salt
1 teaspoon freshly ground black pepper
1/2 teaspoon cayenne pepper
Basil leaves and Parmesan croutons, for garnish

Special Equipment: *immersion blender*

Reserve 1/3 cup of the tomatoes and 1/3 cup of the cucumber for toppings. Combine the remaining tomatoes and cucumber with the next seven ingredients in a large bowl or food processor. Add the sour cream, anchovy paste, salt, black pepper and cayenne pepper. Process with an immersion blender or food processor until smooth. Serve immediately or chill until serving time. Top servings with the reserved tomatoes and cucumber. Garnish with additional basil leaves and Parmesan croutons.

Brunch and Breads

The 1940s proved an extremely active decade for the JLSF as we supported World War II efforts with over 175,000 hours in service. Volunteer opportunities included the Red Cross Motor Corps, the Gray Ladies Services, the American Women's Volunteer Services, the Army Interceptor Command, the Blood Bank, and canteens. In 1946, together with the Community Chest (now the United Way), we organized The Volunteer Bureau of San Francisco, the city's central placement agency. To help finance our community service initiatives, in 1949 we opened the Next-to-New Shop on Fillmore Street, selling nearly new clothing donated by JLSF members and friends. The Next-to-New Shop served as the principal source of income for the Community Trust Fund. At the end of the decade, we instituted our Symphony and Opera Previews, which later expanded to include Ballet and Theater Previews.

As for brunch innovations, San Francisco lays claim to at least two egg dishes, although neither necessarily originated in the 1940s. If you have ever seen Joe's Special on a menu, it was created in San Francisco at New Joe's Restaurant. One night in 1932, when a late-night musician crowd came to eat, the chef could find only spinach, onions, mushrooms, hamburger meat, and eggs, and Joe's Special was born. Showcasing proximity to the Pacific Ocean, Hangtown Fry—a scramble made of eggs, oysters, and bacon—harkens back to the Gold Rush days where the town of Placerville, also known as Hangtown, made the dish famous. As for the unlikely egg-oyster combination, varying legends say that either a wealthy gold miner or a doomed man seeking to postpone his last meal requested the oysters be delivered from San Francisco.

In food politics, San Franciscans participated in the war effort by plowing and planting Victory Gardens from City Hall to Golden Gate Park. While residents had built such gardens in World War I, the effort greatly expanded during World War II, with 250 plots cultivated in Golden Gate Park alone. Producing a significant portion of the city's vegetables, Victory Gardens led to the development of the first farmers' market within San Francisco city limits. First opened in 1943, at the intersection at Market Street & Duboce Avenue, the farmers' market redistributed surplus produce from local farmers to city residents. After the war, residents voted for a permanent market in the Bayshore district, after which Alemany Farmers' Market established operations at its current location in 1947. At the close of the war, San Francisco hosted the international conference that established the United Nations, with its official charter signed on June 26, 1945, at the Civic Center. UN Plaza commemorates the historic occasion.

1941–1950

Open-Face Italian Sausage Omelet

Courtesy of Chef Andrea Froncillo, Franciscan Crab

SERVES 4 TO 6

6 eggs
1/2 cup half-and-half
1/2 cup (2 ounces) shredded mozzarella cheese
Salt and pepper to taste
1 tablespoon olive oil
2 Italian sausages, casings removed and
   sausage chopped
4 slices pancetta or bacon, chopped
1/4 cup chopped green onions
1/2 cup chopped tomato
1/2 avocado, sliced
4 fresh basil leaves
1 tablespoon grated Parmigiano cheese

Special Equipment: *ovenproof 9-inch skillet*

Preheat the broiler. Whisk the eggs with the half-and-half in a bowl. Whisk in the mozzarella cheese and season with salt and pepper.

Heat the olive oil in an ovenproof 9-inch skillet. Add the sausage and sauté for 5 minutes. Add the pancetta and green onions. Reduce the heat and sauté for 2 minutes longer. Stir in the tomato and egg mixture. Cook until soft-set, stirring with a spatula or wooden spoon. Top with the avocado and basil.

Sprinkle with the Parmigiano cheese and broil for 4 to 5 minutes or until light brown. Let stand for 1 to 2 minutes before serving.

FARMERS' MARKET FRITTATA

SERVES 6 TO 8

6 eggs
6 egg whites
1/4 cup half-and-half
Salt and freshly ground pepper to taste
1 tablespoon butter
5 unpeeled small red potatoes, cut into 1/2-inch chunks
1 teaspoon chopped fresh rosemary
1 1/2 teaspoons olive oil
4 shallots, thinly sliced
1 cup (1/4-inch diagonal slices) asparagus
1 cup (1/2-inch pieces) mushrooms
3/4 cup (3 ounces) shredded aged asiago cheese
1/4 cup (1 ounce) grated aged Parmesan cheese
3 vine-ripened tomatoes, seeded and chopped
1/4 cup fresh basil, julienned

Special Equipment: *ovenproof sauté pan*

Whisk the eggs, egg whites and half-and-half in a mixing bowl. Season generously with salt and pepper. Melt the butter in a large ovenproof sauté pan over medium heat. Add the potatoes and season with the rosemary, salt and pepper. Sauté for 10 minutes. Remove to a medium bowl.

Heat the olive oil in the same sauté pan over medium-high heat. Add the shallots and sauté for 4 minutes or until golden brown. Add the asparagus and sauté for 2 minutes. Add the mushrooms and season with salt and pepper. Sauté for 5 minutes longer.

Reduce the heat to low and add the potatoes, the egg mixture and the asiago cheese; mix well. Cook for 5 minutes without stirring.

Preheat the broiler. Sprinkle the frittata with the Parmesan cheese and broil for 3 minutes or until the top is bubbly and brown. Sprinkle the tomatoes and basil over the top and serve.

CHEF'S TIP: Substitute your favorite seasonable green vegetable for asparagus when it is not in season, or use yellow onions instead of shallots. You can also add savory meats.

THIS PAGE GRACIOUSLY SPONSORED BY MICHELLE NICOLE BRANCH

Asparagus and Roasted Red Pepper Strata

SERVES 12

1 pound asparagus, trimmed and
    cut into 1-inch pieces
1 large loaf or 2 small loaves Pugliese or
    other crusty bread
2 cups (8 ounces) shredded fontina cheese
2 cups (8 ounces) grated Gruyère cheese
1 bunch green onions, finely chopped
    (white and light green portions only)
1 or 2 (8-ounce) jars roasted red peppers,
    drained and finely chopped
12 eggs
3 1/2 cups milk
1 tablespoon Dijon mustard
1/2 teaspoon salt
1/2 teaspoon freshly ground pepper

Blanch the asparagus in boiling water in a saucepan for 3 minutes or just until tender. Drain and plunge into ice water to stop the cooking process; drain again.

Spray a 9×13-inch baking dish with nonstick cooking spray. Cut the crusts from the bread and cut into 1-inch cubes. Layer half the bread cubes, 1 cup of the fontina cheese, 1 cup of the Gruyère cheese and half the asparagus, green onions and roasted red peppers in the prepared dish.

Add the remaining bread cubes. Sprinkle with 1/2 cup fontina cheese and 1/2 cup Gruyère cheese and layer with the remaining asparagus, green onions and roasted red peppers.

Combine the eggs, milk, Dijon mustard, salt and pepper in a large bowl and whisk until smooth. Pour over the layers in the baking dish. Cover with plastic wrap and chill in the refrigerator for 4 to 12 hours.

Preheat the oven to 350 degrees. Let the strata stand at room temperature for 30 minutes. Sprinkle with the remaining fontina cheese and Gruyère cheese. Bake, uncovered, for 1 hour or until golden brown and cooked through. Let stand for 10 minutes before serving.

CHEF'S TIP: Add sausage to the strata for a heartier dish or substitute cooked spinach, artichokes, or sun-dried tomatoes for the asparagus when it is not in season.

This page graciously sponsored by Michelle & Kristian McCabe

Sonoma Soufflé

Courtesy of Chuck Williams, founder of Williams-Sonoma
The Sonoma Soufflé originally appeared in The Williams-Sonoma Cookbook with a Guide to Kitchenware.

PAIRS WELL WITH GLORIA FERRER BLANC DE BLANCS

SERVES 4

¹/₂ cup each heavy cream and milk
2 tablespoons unsalted butter
2 tablespoons all-purpose flour
4 egg yolks
1 cup finely chopped cooked shrimp
1 tablespoon each madeira and lemon juice
¹/₂ teaspoon salt
Freshly ground black pepper to taste
Pinch of cayenne pepper
5 egg whites

Special Equipment: *1¹/₂-quart soufflé dish*

Preheat the oven to 350 degrees. Cut a strip of baking parchment or foil and wrap around the outside of an unbuttered 1¹/₂-quart soufflé dish to form a collar above the rim; secure with a pin, paper clip or kitchen twine. Combine the heavy cream and milk in a saucepan. Heat just until warm.

Melt the butter in a saucepan over medium-low heat. Stir in the flour and cook for 2 minutes, stirring vigorously with a wooden spoon or whisk. Add the heated cream mixture and cook over low heat for 3 minutes or until smooth and thickened, stirring constantly. Cool for 5 minutes.

Beat the egg yolks lightly in a bowl. Stir a small amount of the sauce into the egg yolks; stir the egg yolks into the sauce. Add the shrimp, wine, lemon juice, salt, black pepper and cayenne pepper; mix well.

Beat the egg whites in a bowl until soft peaks form. Stir one-fourth of the egg whites into the sauce. Fold the sauce into the egg whites. Spoon into the prepared dish.

Bake for 35 minutes or just until set in the center and light brown. Remove the collar gently and serve immediately.

CHEF'S TIP: Do not omit the madeira; the alcohol will help the soufflé to rise without fail.

Sonoma-Carneros—
Right in Our Own Backyard

Sonoma-Carneros is the first wine region to receive an AVA designation based on climate rather than political boundaries. Sonoma-Carneros is distinguished by a long growing season that coaxes grapes to maturity slowly and consistently. Long known for its unassailable chardonnays, elegant pinot noirs, and effervescent sparkling wines, Sonoma-Carneros is just forty miles north of San Francisco. Gloria Ferrer's Vista Terrace, with unparalleled views of Sonoma-Carneros, is the perfect place to enjoy an afternoon of pinot noir–inspired sparkling and still wines.

OLD-FASHIONED SOURDOUGH PANCAKES

Sourdough is very San Francisco. The starter recipe used to make these pancakes originally appeared in San Francisco a la Carte, the first cookbook published by The Junior League of San Francisco, Inc.

PAIRS WELL WITH MIMOSAS

SERVES 4 TO 6

Sourdough Starter
1 package (1 tablespoon) dry yeast
2 1/2 cups warm water (110 degrees)
2 cups unsifted all-purpose flour
1 tablespoon sugar

Pancakes
1 cup all-purpose flour
1 cup water
1/4 cup olive oil
2 tablespoons sugar
1 egg
1/2 teaspoon salt
1 teaspoon baking soda
1 tablespoon warm water

Special Equipment: *cheesecloth, griddle*

Starter
Soften the yeast in 1/2 cup of the warm water in a 6-cup glass or ceramic bowl. Stir in the remaining 2 cups water, the flour and sugar; beat until smooth. Fold cheesecloth into several thicknesses and cover the bowl. Let stand at room temperature for 5 to 10 days or until the mixture is bubbly and has a sour aroma. Store in the refrigerator after fermentation until needed.

Pancakes
Remove the starter from the refrigerator and combine with the flour and 1 cup water in a bowl; mix well. Cover with a cloth and let stand in a warm place overnight. Remove 2 cups of the starter for the pancakes. Combine with the olive oil, sugar, egg and salt in a large bowl; mix well. Blend the baking soda with 1 tablespoon water in a cup. Fold into the batter; do not beat. Let stand for 1 to 2 minutes or until bubbly and foamy. Heat a lightly buttered griddle until fairly hot. Ladle 1/4 to 1/2 cup batter for each pancake onto the griddle. Cook pancakes for 2 minutes or until bubbles begin to appear and the bottom is brown, checking the bottom with a spatula. Turn the pancakes over and cook until brown. Serve with maple syrup.

CHEF'S TIP: You do have to plan in advance if you want to make these pancakes, especially if you do not have sourdough starter on hand, as the starter takes 5 to 10 days to make.

Keep the Starter Going

Keep the starter going by adding 3/4 cup water, 3/4 cup all-purpose flour and 1 teaspoon sugar for each cup of starter removed and mix well. Let stand at room temperature for 1 day or longer until bubbly. Stir in 1 teaspoon sugar and place, covered, in the refrigerator if not used within 10 days. Continue to add 1 teaspoon sugar every 10 days.

CREAMY GRITS WITH APPLES AND PANCETTA

SERVES 4

6 slices pancetta or bacon, cut into 1/4-inch pieces
1/4 cup water
3 Golden Delicious apples, Granny Smith apples or
   pippin apples, peeled and sliced
1 cup milk
1 tablespoon butter
Pinch of salt
3 cups water
3/4 cup quick-cooking grits
3 tablespoons crumbled feta cheese

Sauté the pancetta in a skillet over medium heat for
5 minutes or until brown. Remove with a slotted spoon.
Add 1/4 cup water and the apples to the skillet and cook
over medium heat for 10 minutes or until tender.

Combine the milk, butter, salt and 3 cups water in a
saucepan and bring to a boil. Stir in the grits and simmer
for 5 minutes, stirring frequently. Add the pancetta and
cook for 2 minutes longer.

Remove from the heat and stir in the cheese until melted.
Spoon into serving bowls and top with the apples.

SUNDAY FRENCH TOAST

Rich and delicious—perfect for a lazy Sunday morning.

SERVES 8

12 eggs
1/2 cup milk
2 tablespoons vanilla extract
1 teaspoon ground cinnamon
1/2 teaspoon ground nutmeg
1 loaf challah or brioche, cut into 1-inch slices
Butter

Whisk the eggs with the milk, vanilla, cinnamon and
nutmeg in a large bowl until smooth. Place one slice of bread
at a time in the mixture, turning to coat both sides. Press
the air out of the center of the bread with your fingers
to saturate the bread, but do not allow it to become soggy.

Melt enough butter to cover the bottom of a sauté pan
or skillet over medium heat. Add the bread slice and cook
until golden brown on both sides. Press with a spatula
until no liquid is expressed to sizzle in the pan. Repeat with
the remaining bread slices. Serve warm with maple syrup,
butter and confectioners' sugar

Mimosas

*When making mimosas, be sure to spend your
money on the orange juice, not just the sparkling
wine. Any sparkling wine with freshly squeezed
naval orange juice is wonderful!*

THIS PAGE GRACIOUSLY SPONSORED BY KATHRYN & PETER COLOSI

Cable Car Morning Muffins

SERVES 12

3/4 cup whole wheat flour
1/2 cup wheat bran
2 tablespoons wheat germ
1/2 cup packed brown sugar
1/4 cup rolled oats
1/2 teaspoon plus 1/8 teaspoon baking soda
2 tablespoons ground cinnamon
Dash of nutmeg
1/8 teaspoon salt
3/4 cup skim milk
1 egg
2 tablespoons canola oil
1 tablespoon vanilla extract
3/4 cup pecans, chopped
1/2 cup golden raisins
1/2 cup shredded carrots
1/2 cup chopped Golden Delicious apple, Granny Smith
  apple or pippin apple
1/2 cup fresh blackberries

Preheat the oven to 350 degrees. Combine the whole wheat flour, wheat bran, wheat germ, brown sugar, oats, baking soda, cinnamon, nutmeg and salt in a large bowl. Add the skim milk, egg, canola oil and vanilla; mix well. Stir in the pecans, raisins, carrots, apple and blackberries. Spoon into paper-lined muffin cups. Bake for 20 minutes or until a wooden pick inserted into the center comes out clean.

CHEF'S TIP: You can substitute ground flax for the wheat germ, dried cranberries or dates for the raisins, and when in season, peaches for the apples.

Banana Bread

MAKES 1 LOAF

1 1/4 cups all-purpose flour
1 teaspoon baking soda
1 teaspoon ground cinnamon
1/2 teaspoon salt
1 cup sugar
1/2 cup (1 stick) butter, softened
1/2 teaspoon vanilla extract
3 ripe bananas, mashed
2 eggs, at room temperature and beaten

Preheat the oven to 350 degrees. Sift the flour, baking soda, cinnamon and salt together. Cream the sugar, butter and vanilla in a mixing bowl until light and fluffy. Add the bananas; mix well. Beat in the eggs. Add the dry ingredients and mix just until moistened; do not overmix.

Spoon into a lightly greased loaf pan. Bake for 45 minutes or until set and the edges pull away from the sides of the pan. Cool in the pan on a wire rack for 10 minutes, then remove from the pan to cool completely.

CHEF'S TIP: Very ripe bananas work best in banana bread. You can freeze the bananas in their peels and thaw just before needed.

Cardamom Bread

MAKES 2 LARGE LOAVES

Cardamom Bread

1 cup milk
1 package dry yeast
1/4 cup warm water (110 degrees)
1/2 cup sugar
2 eggs, lightly beaten
1/2 teaspoon ground cardamom
1 teaspoon salt
4 to 4 1/2 cups all-purpose flour
1/4 cup (1/2 stick) butter, melted

Glaze and Topping

1 egg
2 tablespoons milk
1 teaspoon water
1/4 cup sugar
1/4 teaspoon cinnamon
1/4 cup sliced almonds or crushed walnuts

Special Equipment: *stand mixer with a dough hook*

Bread

Heat the milk in a saucepan over medium heat just until bubbles begin to form around the edge and the mixture is steamy. Cool to room temperature.

Mix the yeast into the water in the bowl of a stand mixer fitted with a dough hook. Let stand for 5 minutes to soften. Add the milk, sugar, eggs, cardamom, salt and 2 cups of the flour; beat until smooth. Beat in the butter. Add enough of the remaining flour gradually to form a stiff dough, beating until well mixed.

Place on a lightly floured work surface and cover with a dry cloth. Let rest for 5 to 15 minutes. Knead for 10 minutes or until smooth and elastic, adding additional flour as needed.

Place the dough in a greased bowl, turning to grease all sides. Cover and let rise in a warm place for 1 1/2 to 2 hours or until doubled in bulk. Punch down the dough, cover and let rise for 45 minutes or until doubled in bulk.

Place on a lightly oiled work surface and divide into two portions. Work with one portion at a time, dividing it into three equal portions. Roll the portions on the work surface with oiled hands to form three 30-inch ropes. Braid to form a loaf; pinch the ends to seal and tuck under. Shape each braid into a circle on separate greased baking sheets. Repeat with the remaining dough. Let rise for 45 to 60 minutes or until doubled in bulk.

Glaze and Topping

Beat the egg with the milk and water in a small bowl. Mix the sugar with the cinnamon in a small bowl. Brush the egg mixture over the loaves with a pastry brush; sprinkle with the almonds and cinnamon-sugar.

To bake, preheat the oven to 375 degrees. Bake the loaves for 25 to 30 minutes or just until the crust is light brown and tender, but not crisp. Remove to wire racks to cool. Serve warm or at room temperature.

Vegetables and Sides

The 1950s witnessed the expansion of the JLSF programs. In 1954, the JLSF convened our first Community Advisory Committee, comprised of an array of San Francisco's best and brightest community leaders in collaboration with the JLSF. In the next year, the Chrysler Corporation helped the JLSF raise over $21,000 by co-sponsoring the original musical comedy *The Forward Look*. Collaborating with the National Foundation for Junior Museums, members also co-founded the Coyote Point Museum for Environmental Education.

San Francisco's Celery Victor, created by the prolific Chef Victor Hirtzler, may be the vegetable dish for which the city is most credited, but it is certainly not a vegetarian dish! Complexity marked luxury hotel cuisine in the first half of the century, as the recipe calls for boiling the celery in an enhanced chicken and veal stock. The practice was thought to remove the bitter vegetal taste, imparting the green stalks with sweet delicate flavors. For the home cook, Rice-a-Roni® debuted its quick-cooking side dish for busy housewives in 1958. The first "San Francisco treat" was comprised of rice, vermicelli, and chicken bouillon and was marketed by the DeDomenico pasta-making family, who, at the turn of the century, had emigrated from Italy to San Francisco's Mission District.

During the 1950s, the San Francisco cultural and literary renaissance known as the Beat Culture ensued. The philosophy's leading characters, Allen Ginsberg and Jack Kerouac, could be found writing and reading their poetry at North Beach coffee shops and bookstores like City Lights, which was established in 1953 by the literary critic Lawrence Ferlinghetti. One of the seminal moments in the Beat movement occurred at Six Gallery, when Ginsberg performed his controversial poem *Howl* during a poetry slam.

1951–1960

Wild Rice with Mushrooms and Water Chestnuts

SERVES 6 TO 8

1 tablespoon dried parsley
2 teaspoons Italian
   seasoning
1/2 teaspoon dried thyme
1/2 teaspoon dried oregano
1/2 teaspoon turmeric
1/4 teaspoon garlic powder
1/4 teaspoon ground cumin
1/4 teaspoon paprika
1 teaspoon salt
1/2 teaspoon freshly
   ground pepper
1 cup wild rice blend
1 1/2 cups chicken broth

1/2 cup slivered almonds
1/2 cup (1 stick)
   unsalted butter
3 ribs celery, finely chopped
1 yellow onion, finely chopped
4 ounces fresh mushrooms,
   thinly sliced
2 garlic cloves, minced
1 (5-ounce) can sliced
   water chestnuts, drained
   and chopped
2 tablespoons low-sodium
   soy sauce

Combine the parsley, Italian seasoning, thyme, oregano, turmeric, garlic powder, cumin, paprika, salt and pepper in a bowl; mix well.

Preheat the oven to 350 degrees. Combine the rice, broth and spice mix in a medium saucepan; mix well. Bring to a boil over medium-high heat; stir and cover. Reduce the heat and cook using the rice package directions.

Sauté the almonds in 1 tablespoon of the butter in a large skillet for 3 minutes or until light brown. Remove the almonds with a slotted spoon. Melt the remaining butter in the skillet. Add the celery, onion, mushrooms and garlic and sauté for 5 minutes. Add the water chestnuts and sauté for 2 minutes longer.

Combine the vegetables with the rice, almonds and soy sauce in a bowl; mix well. Spoon into a greased 2 1/2-quart baking dish. Bake for 30 minutes or until heated through.

STUFFED ARTICHOKES

California artichokes are usually available year-round, but they are at their peak from spring through fall.

PAIRS WELL WITH SAM ADAMS LIGHT

SERVES 4

4 large artichokes
Salt to taste
2 lemons, cut into halves
1 (10-ounce) log goat
   cheese, at room
   temperature
2 tablespoons heavy cream
2 tablespoons chopped
   fresh basil

1 garlic clove, minced
1/2 tablespoon minced fresh
   flat-leaf parsley
1/2 teaspoon each salt and
   freshly ground pepper
1/4 cup bread crumbs
1/2 tablespoon minced fresh
   flat-leaf parsley
1 tablespoon olive oil

Slice off the stem end and top inch of each artichoke. Cut off the tips of each leaf with kitchen shears. Bring a stockpot of salted water to a boil. Squeeze the lemon juice into the stockpot and add the lemon halves. Add the artichokes and cook for 30 minutes. Drain the artichokes stem end up on a kitchen towel; cool. Combine the cheese, cream, basil, garlic, 1/2 tablespoon parsley, 1/2 teaspoon salt and pepper in a bowl; mix well. Mix the bread crumbs with 1/2 tablespoon parsley in a bowl.

Preheat the oven to 400 degrees. Spread the artichokes open and scrape out the fuzzy chokes. Spoon 2 to 3 tablespoons of the cheese mixture into each artichoke. Arrange in a roasting pan and sprinkle with the bread crumb mixture; drizzle with the olive oil. Bake for 25 minutes or until heated through. Serve warm.

CHEF'S TIP: For smaller portions, cut the artichokes into halves lengthwise. Remove the chokes and spoon the stuffing into the center of each artichoke half. Bake as above.

SMOKED MOZZARELLA MASHED POTATOES AND CORN

SERVES 8

3 cups fresh corn kernels (about 6 ears)
2 1/2 pounds red potatoes, peeled and cut into quarters
3/4 cup half-and-half
1/2 cup (2 ounces) shredded cold-smoked mozzarella cheese
3 tablespoons butter, softened
1/4 cup chopped fresh cilantro
1 tablespoon lime juice
3/4 teaspoon salt
1/2 teaspoon freshly ground pepper

Spray a large nonstick skillet with cooking spray and heat over medium-high heat. Add the corn and sauté for 5 minutes or until light brown. Cool to room temperature.

Combine the potatoes with enough water to cover in a stockpot. Bring to a boil over high heat. Reduce the heat to low and simmer for 15 minutes or until tender; drain and return the potatoes to the stockpot. Add the half-and-half, cheese and butter. Mash until no large lumps remain.

Cook over low heat for 2 minutes or until heated through, stirring constantly. Stir in the corn, cilantro, lime juice, salt and pepper. Serve hot.

CHEF'S TIP: The smoked mozzarella adds depth to this dish, but regular mozzarella can be substituted. To re-create the smoky flavor, add a few dashes of liquid smoke with the cheese. You can also substitute thawed and drained frozen corn for the fresh corn.

Brussels Sprouts with Crispy Pancetta

PAIRS WELL WITH SAMUEL ADAMS NOBLE PILSNER

SERVES 4

Salt to taste
1 pound fresh brussels sprouts, trimmed
3 tablespoons extra-virgin olive oil
1/2 small yellow onion, chopped
4 ounces pancetta, cut into 1/4-inch pieces
4 garlic cloves, minced
1 cup low-sodium chicken broth
3 tablespoons balsamic vinegar
1/4 cup (1/2 stick) unsalted butter, chopped
Freshly ground pepper to taste

Bring a large stockpot of salted water to a boil. Add the brussels sprouts and blanch for 5 minutes; drain.

Heat the olive oil in a large cast-iron skillet over medium-high heat. Add the onion, pancetta and garlic and sauté for 5 minutes or until the pancetta is crisp and golden brown. Add the broth, balsamic vinegar and brussels sprouts. Cook for 5 to 10 minutes or until the broth is reduced by two-thirds. Stir in the butter and increase the heat to high. Cook for 4 to 6 minutes or until the brussels sprouts are light brown. Season with salt and pepper and serve immediately.

CHEF'S TIP: To steam whole brussels sprouts, cut an X in the stem to allow them to cook evenly.

Roasted Baby Red Potatoes

SERVES 4

2 tablespoons extra-virgin olive oil
2 teaspoons Greek seasoning
2 teaspoons garlic powder
2 teaspoons onion powder
2 teaspoons dried dill weed
2 teaspoons freshly ground pepper
1 teaspoon salt
10 baby red potatoes, cut into quarters
Paprika to taste

Preheat the oven to 400 degrees. Line a baking sheet with foil and spray with cooking spray.

Whisk the olive oil, Greek seasoning, garlic powder, onion powder, dill weed, pepper and salt in a large bowl. Add the potatoes and toss to coat evenly. Spread in a single layer on the prepared baking sheet and sprinkle with paprika. Bake for 25 to 30 minutes or until tender. Serve warm.

THIS PAGE GRACIOUSLY SPONSORED BY JENNIFER L. JOHNSTON

TARRAGON GREEN BEANS

SERVES 4

1/2 cup (1 stick) butter
1 pound fresh green beans, trimmed
1/2 cup chopped fresh tarragon
1/2 cup chopped fresh parsley
1 tablespoon plus 1 teaspoon salt
2 teaspoons freshly ground pepper

Melt the butter in a medium skillet over medium-high heat. Add the green beans and sauté for 5 minutes or until tender. Add the tarragon, parsley, salt and pepper. Sauté for 1 minute longer and serve warm.

ROASTED CAULIFLOWER AND WALNUTS

SERVES 4

1 large head cauliflower, cut into florets
2 garlic cloves, minced
2 tablespoons walnut oil
1 teaspoon salt
1/2 teaspoon freshly ground pepper
1/2 cup walnuts, chopped

Preheat the oven to 400 degrees. Spread the cauliflower florets in a single layer in a lightly oiled 9×13-inch baking dish. Sprinkle with the garlic and drizzle evenly with the walnut oil. Season with the salt and pepper. Bake for 15 minutes. Top with the chopped walnuts and bake for 10 minutes longer or until the top is light brown. Serve warm.

GARLIC AND HERB TOMATOES

SERVES 6

3 tablespoons olive oil
2 garlic cloves, minced
2 pints cherry tomatoes or grape tomatoes
2 tablespoons chopped fresh basil
2 tablespoons chopped fresh flat-leaf parsley
2 teaspoons chopped fresh thyme leaves
1 teaspoon kosher salt
1/4 teaspoon freshly ground pepper
Chopped fresh basil and flat-leaf parsley, for garnish

Heat the olive oil in a large sauté pan over medium heat. Add the garlic and sauté for 30 seconds. Spread the tomatoes in a single layer in the sauté pan and sprinkle with 2 tablespoons basil, 2 tablespoons parsley, the thyme, kosher salt and pepper. Reduce the heat to low and cook for 5 to 7 minutes or until the tomatoes begin to lose their firm round shape, tossing occasionally. Garnish with additional chopped basil and parsley. Serve warm or at room temperature.

THIS PAGE GRACIOUSLY SPONSORED BY KATIE BORZCIK

Fried Green Tomatoes with Roasted Grapes and Goat Cheese

Courtesy of Chef Mark Gorden, Terzo

SERVES 8

4 large organic green tomatoes
Fleur de sel or other coarse salt
1 cup coarsely ground cornmeal
1/2 cup all-purpose flour
1 tablespoon cornstarch
1/4 cup olive oil
8 small bunches organic seedless red grapes
8 ounces crumbled goat cheese
Additional olive oil

Preheat the oven to 425 degrees. Core each tomato and cut into four 1/2-inch slices, discarding the ends. Season with Fleur de Sel salt. Mix the cornmeal with the flour and cornstarch in a bowl. Add the tomato slices and toss to coat well.

Heat 1/4 cup olive oil in a medium saucepan over medium heat until hot but not smoking. Shake any excess cornmeal mixture from the tomato slices gently and add to the saucepan in batches. Sauté for 3 minutes or until golden brown. Turn the slices and sauté for 2 to 3 minutes longer. Remove to serving plates with a spatula, placing two slices on each plate. Tent with foil to keep warm.

Toss the grapes gently with olive oil and coarse salt in a bowl. Arrange on a baking sheet lined with baking parchment. Bake for 3 minutes or just until hot. Add one bunch to each plate. Crumble the cheese over the tomatoes and grapes and sprinkle with the coarse salt. Drizzle with additional olive oil. Serve immediately.

Sautéed Mushrooms with Sherry

SERVES 2 TO 4

2 1/2 cups quartered small white mushrooms
6 garlic cloves, minced
2 green onions, chopped
1/4 cup olive oil
1/2 cup dry Spanish sherry
1 tablespoon sherry vinegar
1 tablespoon fresh thyme leaves
Juice of 1/4 lemon
1/4 teaspoon paprika
1 teaspoon salt
1/2 teaspoon freshly ground black pepper
1/2 teaspoon crushed red pepper flakes
Thyme leaves, for garnish

Sauté the mushrooms, garlic and green onions in the olive oil in a skillet over medium heat for 2 minutes, stirring constantly. Stir in the sherry, sherry vinegar, 1 tablespoon thyme, the lemon juice, paprika, salt, black pepper and red pepper flakes. Simmer for 5 minutes or until the alcohol has evaporated and the mushrooms are tender. Garnish with additional thyme. Serve hot with crusty bread.

CHEF'S TIP: To prevent flaming up, remove the skillet from the heat when adding the Spanish sherry if using gas burners.

California Couscous

This versatile side dish is chock full of healthy and delicious fruits and nuts.

SERVES 6 TO 8

1 1/2 cups chicken broth or vegetable stock
1 teaspoon extra-virgin olive oil
1 cup couscous
2/3 cup chopped pitted dates
1/2 cup slivered almonds, toasted
1 (15-ounce) can garbanzo beans, drained
1/2 cup minced green onions
1/3 cup chopped fresh chives
1/4 cup extra-virgin olive oil
Juice of 1 lemon
1 teaspoon ground cardamom
Salt and freshly ground pepper to taste

Bring the broth and 1 teaspoon olive oil to a boil in a medium saucepan. Stir in the couscous and remove from the heat. Cover and let stand for 5 minutes. Spoon into a large bowl and cool. Add the dates, almonds, garbanzo beans, green onions and chives; mix well.

Whisk 1/4 cup olive oil with the lemon juice and cardamom in a small bowl. Season with salt and pepper. Drizzle over the couscous and mix well. Let stand at room temperature for 1 hour to blend the flavors before serving.

CHEF'S TIP: California dates are available year-round. Although most people believe dates are a dried fruit, they are fresh and will keep in an airtight container at room temperature for two months. Other dried fruits, such as apricots, cranberries, and golden raisins, can be substituted for the dates in this recipe.

Sourdough and Fennel Stuffing

SERVES 12

6 cups (1-inch cubes) Boudin Bakery sourdough bread
1 pound Italian sausage, casings removed and sausage crumbled
5 tablespoons butter
1 cup chopped white onion
2 ribs celery, chopped
1 fennel bulb, thinly sliced
1/8 teaspoon salt
1/4 teaspoon freshly ground pepper
1 tablespoon chopped fresh sage
2 eggs, lightly beaten
1 cup chicken broth
Olive oil

Preheat the oven to 400 degrees. Spread the bread cubes on a rimmed baking sheet. Toast for 3 minutes. Turn the bread cubes and toast for 3 to 5 minutes longer or until golden brown. Remove to a large bowl.

Reduce the oven temperature to 350 degrees. Sauté the sausage in a large skillet over medium-high heat for 8 to 10 minutes or until cooked through. Remove to the bowl with the bread cubes with a slotted spoon.

Add the butter to the drippings in the skillet. Add the onion, celery, fennel, salt and pepper. Sauté for 10 minutes or until the vegetables are tender. Add the sage and cook for 5 minutes longer. Add to the bread mixture. Stir in the eggs and broth and drizzle with olive oil.

Spoon into a 9×13-inch baking pan sprayed with nonstick cooking spray. Cover with foil and bake for 30 minutes or until heated through. Uncover and bake for 15 minutes longer. Serve warm.

Vegetarian

By the 1960s, the JLSF had gained wide recognition as an established community leader and celebrated its fiftieth anniversary in 1961. To commemorate the occasion, Mayor George Christopher declared an official Junior League Day, which was highlighted by a community leaders' luncheon and a ball to honor past presidents. In 1968, after five years of research, the JLSF volunteers published *Here Today*, a definitive study of historically and architecturally significant pre-1920 buildings in San Francisco, San Mateo, and Marin Counties.

Inspired by the counter-culture movement and its turn to environmentalism, vegetable-based diets took root in San Francisco in the 1960s. Macrobiotic, pure vegetarian, and organic practices proliferated due to the rejection of capitalist and corporate values by the counter-culture and antiwar peace movements, the basis of which emanated from the San Francisco youth culture iconically captured in the Haight-Ashbury "Summer of Love." Looking for nonmeat diets, San Franciscans became aware of the diverse ethnic cuisines available in close proximity. As grain- and vegetable-based cuisines grew more popular, many San Franciscans took greater interest in the Mexican and Chinese food customs surrounding them.

Several historians trace the popularity of the Mission District's taquerias to the 1960s. Transitioning from an Irish to a Latino community during this era, the Mission boasted restaurants, music, and nightlife from Central and South American immigrants. Many of the neighborhood's signature murals were painted in this decade. During a time of increasing intercultural exploration and changing dietary practices, burritos satisfied the craving. Vegetables, rice, beans, and salsa wrapped in tortillas comprised a complete meal, made even more decadent with guacamole.

In Chinese cuisine, chop suey best tells the story of cultural exchange. Introduced to San Francisco by Chinese chefs during the Gold Rush, this dish, whose name literally means "odds and ends," satisfied the tastes of white gold miners—and has since traveled the world. In the 1960s, a largely vegetarian Chinese cuisine was repopularized during the same time that Chinatown witnessed neighborhood revitalization with a wave of new arrivals from distant shores, further infusing American Chinese food with mainland Chinese and Taiwanese cooking techniques. Upscale and ambitious Chinese restaurants like Chef Cecilia Chiang's The Mandarin, which opened in 1961, elevated the culinary experience beyond chop suey to rave reviews by food critics, forever changing San Francisco's relationship to Chinese cuisine.

1961–1970

Southwestern Black Bean Cakes with Chipotle Sauce

Courtesy of Chef Laurie Gauguin, private chef

SERVES 4

1 canned chipotle chile in adobo sauce
1/2 cup plain yogurt
Salt to taste
1 (15-ounce) can black beans, drained and rinsed
1/2 cup finely chopped onion
3/4 cup finely chopped red bell pepper
2 garlic cloves, minced
1 tablespoon olive oil
1/2 cup fresh corn kernels
1/4 cup chopped fresh cilantro
1 tablespoon finely grated lime zest
2 teaspoons chili powder
1 egg white
1/2 cup panko (Japanese bread crumbs)
2 tablespoons olive oil

Process the chipotle chile with the yogurt in a food processor until smooth. Season with salt. Chill in the refrigerator. Rinse the food processor bowl and add the black beans; pulse until coarsely chopped. Spoon into a medium bowl. Sauté the onion, bell pepper and garlic in 1 tablespoon olive oil in a medium skillet over medium heat for 3 to 4 minutes or until the onion is translucent. Add to the beans. Stir in the corn, cilantro, lime zest, chili powder and salt. Scoop into four portions and shape into cakes.

Whisk the egg whites in a bowl until frothy. Brush on the bean cakes with a pastry brush. Coat well with the panko. Heat 2 tablespoons olive oil in a medium skillet over medium-low heat. Add the cakes and sauté for 5 minutes on each side or until brown. Serve with the chipotle sauce.

Spring Risotto

This is a very versatile dish, as other vegetables can be substituted to best utilize the season's harvest.

SERVES 6

3/4 cup mascarpone cheese
2 tablespoons lemon juice
5 cups chicken stock
1 1/2 tablespoons olive oil
1 1/2 tablespoons unsalted butter
3 cups chopped leeks (white and light green portions only)
1 cup chopped fennel bulb
1 1/2 cups arborio rice
2/3 cup dry white wine
1 pound thin asparagus, blanched and chopped into
   1-inch pieces
1 3/4 cups fresh shelled peas, or 1 (10-ounce) package
   frozen peas, thawed
Grated zest of 2 lemons
2 teaspoons kosher salt
1 teaspoon freshly ground pepper
1/2 cup (2 ounces) grated Parmesan cheese
1 teaspoon kosher salt
1/2 teaspoon freshly ground pepper
Olive oil for drizzling

Whisk the mascarpone cheese with the lemon juice in a small bowl. Heat the stock in a saucepan.

Heat 1 1/2 tablespoons olive oil and the butter in a Dutch oven or large heavy saucepan over medium heat. Add the leeks and fennel and sauté for 5 to 7 minutes or until tender. Add the rice and sauté, stirring to coat well. Stir in the wine and simmer over low heat until most of the wine has been absorbed, stirring constantly.

Add the stock two ladles at a time, cooking until most of the liquid has been absorbed after each addition and stirring frequently; the cooking time will be about 30 minutes. Add the asparagus, peas, lemon zest, 2 teaspoons kosher salt and 1 teaspoon pepper when the rice appears nearly tender. Cook until the rice is tender but still firm. Remove from the heat and stir in the mascarpone mixture. Sprinkle with the Parmesan cheese, 1 teaspoon kosher salt and 1/2 teaspoon pepper. Drizzle with olive oil.

Arborio Rice

Arborio is a short grain rice named after the town where it is grown in Italy. It is used primarily for risotto. The grain is short, fat, and slightly oval in shape. It produces risotto with a firm, creamy, and chewy texture due to the high starch content and blends well with other flavors. Today it is grown in California and Texas.

This page graciously sponsored by Amie Pfeifer

Quinoa Polenta

Courtesy of Chef/Owner James Schenk, Pisco Latin Lounge

SERVES 10

2/3 cup dried shiitake mushrooms
3 cups water
1 cup white quinoa
1/3 cup heavy cream
2/3 cup grated Parmesan cheese
1/3 cup queso fresco or other semi-firm cow's milk cheese
1 1/2 teaspoons mascarpone cheese
1/8 teaspoon grated fresh nutmeg, or more to taste
1/2 teaspoon salt

Combine the mushrooms with 2 cups of the water in a saucepan. Simmer over low heat for 30 minutes. Remove the mushrooms and finely chop. Reserve the cooking liquid.

Bring the remaining 1 cup water to a boil in a large saucepan. Stir in the quinoa and return to a boil, stirring constantly. Add 2/3 cup of the reserved mushroom cooking liquid and cook for 10 to 12 minutes or until the quinoa is al dente, adding additional cooking liquid as needed to reach the desired consistency.

Reduce the heat and stir in the heavy cream. Add the Parmesan cheese, queso fresco and mascarpone cheese. Cook until the cheeses melt, stirring to blend well. Add the mushrooms to the quinoa and season with the nutmeg and salt.

Sesame Tofu and Soba Noodle Bowls

PAIRS WELL WITH SAKE

SERVES 2

7 ounces firm tofu, cut into 1-inch cubes
3 tablespoons low-sodium soy sauce
2 teaspoons dark sesame oil
1/4 teaspoon ground ginger
3 ounces buckwheat soba noodles
1 teaspoon dark sesame oil
1 garlic clove, minced
1 head bok choy, cut into 1-inch slices
Sesame seeds, for garnish

Drain the tofu on paper towels, pressing lightly to remove excess liquid. Mix the soy sauce, 2 teaspoons sesame oil and the ginger in a medium bowl. Add the tofu and toss to coat well. Marinate for 15 minutes.

Cook the noodles in a saucepan of boiling water using the package directions; drain and keep warm.

Heat 1 teaspoon sesame oil in a medium nonstick sauté pan over medium heat. Add the garlic and sauté for 1 minute. Stir in the bok choy and sauté for 2 minutes. Remove the tofu from the marinade using a slotted spoon and add to the bok choy; reserve the marinade. Cook the tofu for 3 minutes or until light brown, adding additional sesame oil if needed to prevent sticking.

Stir in the noodles and reserved marinade. Cook until heated through, tossing lightly to mix well. Garnish servings with sesame seeds.

CHEF'S TIP: Look for soba noodles in the international aisle of the grocery store.

Green Olive and Garlic Pizza

SERVES 4

Pizza Dough

1 1/2 cups water
1 tablespoon large-flaked sea salt
1 teaspoon confectioners' sugar
1 package rapid-rise dry yeast
1 tablespoon extra-virgin olive oil
4 cups all-purpose flour

Pizza Toppings

4 large garlic cloves, thinly sliced
2 tablespoons extra-virgin olive oil
Olive oil for brushing
20 green olives, coarsely chopped
Crushed red pepper to taste
Smoked sea salt and freshly ground black pepper to taste
16 ounces fresh mozzarella cheese, cut into 1/8-inch slices

Special Equipment: *instant-read thermometer, stand mixer with a paddle attachment, pizza stone*

Dough

Heat the water to 125 degrees on an instant-read thermometer in a small saucepan. Stir in the sea salt and confectioners' sugar until dissolved. Mix in the yeast and olive oil. Let stand at room temperature for 5 minutes or until foamy. Combine with the flour in the bowl of a stand mixer fitted with a paddle attachment; beat at low speed for 10 minutes. Let rest for 10 minutes and then mix for 10 minutes longer.

Place in a lightly oiled large ceramic or glass bowl, turning to coat the surface. Cover with a damp kitchen towel and let rise in a warm place for 2 hours or until doubled in bulk.

Punch down the dough on a lightly floured work surface and divide into four portions. Shape into balls, dust lightly with flour and place 6 inches apart on a large baking sheet. Cover with oiled plastic wrap and let stand for 2 hours.

Pizza

Place a pizza stone on the center oven rack and preheat the oven to 500 degrees for 1 hour. Sauté the garlic in 2 tablespoons olive oil in a small skillet for 4 minutes or until golden brown, shaking the skillet several times.

Roll each ball of dough into an 8-inch circle on a sheet of baking parchment. Stretch each into a 12-inch circle with your hands. Brush lightly with olive oil. Sprinkle with the olives, garlic, crushed red pepper, smoked sea salt and black pepper. Arrange the mozzarella slices over the top.

Preheat the broiler for 5 minutes. Slide the pizzas and baking parchment one at a time onto the heated pizza stone. Broil for 5 minutes or until the bottom crust is crisp and the top is bubbly. Cut into wedges to serve.

CHEF'S TIP: Vary the pizza by adding cooked cubed pancetta, sautéed onions, halved figs, and fontina cheese; garnish with arugula and a drizzle of olive oil. You can substitute 2 1/2 teaspoons kosher salt for the large-flaked sea salt in the dough. Smoked sea salt is flaky and not as salty as table salt.

Tomato Tart

PAIRS WELL WITH ACORN WINERY/ALEGRIA VINEYARDS SANGIOVESE

SERVES 4

3/4 cup whole wheat flour
3/4 cup all-purpose flour
1 tablespoon dried thyme
1/2 teaspoon coarsely ground pepper
4 1/2 tablespoons unsalted butter, chopped and chilled
1/3 cup vegetable shortening, chopped and chilled
1/3 cup ice water
6 plum tomatoes, cut into 1/4-inch slices
Coarse salt to taste
2 cups (8 ounces) shredded Gruyère cheese
2 tablespoons chopped fresh thyme
1 tablespoon chopped fresh Italian parsley
1/2 teaspoon grated nutmeg
1/4 teaspoon coarsely ground pepper
1 tablespoon extra-virgin olive oil

Special Equipment: *Rectangular or 9-inch round tart pan
with removable bottom*

Whisk the whole wheat flour and all-purpose flour in a bowl. Stir in the dried thyme and 1/2 teaspoon pepper. Cut in the butter and shortening to the consistency of coarse meal. Add the ice water 1 tablespoon at a time, mixing with a fork to form a ball. Press into a disc and cover with plastic wrap. Chill in the refrigerator for 3 hours.

Place the tomato slices on a paper towel and sprinkle with coarse salt; let stand for 30 minutes. Pat dry with paper towels. Preheat the oven to 375 degrees.

Roll the dough into a long rectangle 1/8 inch thick. Place in a rectangular tart pan; trim and flute the edges. You can also roll the dough into a circle and place in a 9-inch round tart pan. Prick the crust with a fork and line with foil; fill with pie weights or dried beans. Bake for 10 minutes. Remove the weights and foil and bake for 12 minutes longer. Cool slightly.

Sprinkle the cheese over the tart crust and arrange the tomatoes over the cheese. Sprinkle with the fresh thyme, parsley, nutmeg and 1/4 teaspoon pepper. Drizzle with the olive oil. Bake for 40 minutes.

Let stand at room temperature for 10 minutes. Loosen the tart from the pan with a spatula and remove carefully from the pan.

THIS PAGE GRACIOUSLY SPONSORED BY JENNIFER KURRIE

LINGUINI WITH ARUGULA, RICOTTA SALATA AND SUN-DRIED TOMATOES

Courtesy of Executive Chef Annie Somerville, Greens Restaurant

SERVES 4 TO 6

Salt to taste
8 ounces linguini
3 tablespoons olive oil
6 large shallots, sliced (about 1 cup)
1/2 teaspoon salt
Pinch of freshly ground pepper
1/2 tablespoon minced garlic
12 oil-pack sun-dried tomato halves, thinly sliced
1/4 cup white wine
1 tablespoon olive oil
1/4 teaspoon salt
Pinch of freshly ground pepper
4 to 6 cups arugula leaves
2 ounces crumbled ricotta cheese
1/3 cup pine nuts, toasted
1 tablespoon chopped flat-leaf parsley
1 tablespoon chopped fresh oregano
1 tablespoon chopped fresh marjoram
1 tablespoon chopped fresh thyme
2 ounces crumbled ricotta cheese, for garnish
Grated Parmesan cheese, for garnish

Bring a large saucepan of lightly salted water to a boil and add the pasta. Cook for 10 minutes or just until tender; keep warm. Reserve 1 1/2 cups of the cooking liquid.

Heat 3 tablespoons olive oil in a large sauté pan and add the shallots, 1/2 teaspoon salt and a pinch of pepper. Sauté over medium heat for 3 to 4 minutes or until tender. Add the garlic and sun-dried tomatoes and sauté for 1 minute longer. Stir in the wine and cook for 3 minutes or until the wine has nearly evaporated.

Add the reserved cooking liquid and the pasta to the sauté pan. Stir in 1 tablespoon olive oil, 1/4 teaspoon salt and a pinch of pepper. Cook for 1 minute to reduce the liquid. Add the arugula, 2 ounces ricotta cheese, the pine nuts, parsley, oregano, marjoram and thyme. Cook for 30 seconds or just until the arugula wilts. Adjust the seasonings and serve in warm bowls. Garnish with 2 ounces ricotta cheese and Parmesan cheese.

THIS PAGE GRACIOUSLY SPONSORED BY IRENA MATIJAS

PENNE WITH KALAMATA OLIVES AND CHEESE

SERVES 8

2 cups chopped yellow onions
2 teaspoons minced garlic
3 tablespoons olive oil
2 (28-ounce) cans plum tomatoes with basil
1 teaspoon crushed dried red pepper
2 cups chicken broth
Salt and freshly ground pepper to taste
16 ounces penne
2 tablespoons olive oil
2 1/2 cups (10 ounces) shredded Havarti cheese
1 cup pitted whole kalamata olives
1/2 cup (2 ounces) grated asiago cheese
1/4 cup finely chopped fresh basil, for garnish

Sauté the onions and garlic in 3 tablespoons olive oil in a large saucepan over medium heat until the onion is translucent. Add the tomatoes and crushed red pepper. Bring to a boil, stirring and crushing the tomatoes against the side of the saucepan. Stir in the broth and return to a boil. Reduce the heat and simmer for 1 1/2 hours or until reduced and thickened to the desired consistency, stirring occasionally. Season with salt and pepper.

Preheat the oven to 375 degrees. Cook the pasta al dente using the package directions; drain. Toss with 2 tablespoons olive oil and add to the sauce. Add the Havarti cheese and stir until melted. Mix in 3/4 cup of the olives.

Spoon into a 9×13-inch baking dish and top with the remaining 1/4 cup olives and the asiago cheese. Bake for 30 minutes. Garnish servings with fresh basil.

VEGETABLE CHILI BOWL

SERVES 6

2 white onions, chopped
2 red bell peppers, chopped
3 garlic cloves, minced
1/2 cup olive oil
2 zucchini, chopped
1 tablespoon chili powder
1 tablespoon ground cumin
1 (14-ounce) can peeled tomatoes
Salt and freshly ground pepper to taste
1 (15-ounce) can dark red kidney beans,
    drained and rinsed
1 (15-ounce) can chick-peas, drained and rinsed
1/2 cup each chopped fresh parsley and cilantro
2 tablespoons fresh lemon juice

Toppings
1/2 cup sour cream
1 green bell pepper, chopped
6 ounces Cheddar cheese, shredded
Hot sauce (optional)

Sauté the onions, bell peppers and garlic in the olive oil in a Dutch oven over medium heat for 5 minutes, stirring with a nonmetallic spoon. Add the zucchini and sauté for 3 minutes. Stir in the chili powder and cumin and cook for 1 minute. Add the undrained tomatoes, stirring to break up. Season with salt and pepper. Stir in the kidney beans and chick-peas. Cover and simmer for 15 minutes or until heated through. Add the parsley, cilantro and lemon juice. Provide the sour cream, green bell pepper, Cheddar cheese and hot sauce for topping individual servings.

Seafood

The 1970s witnessed the expansion of the JLSF programs and membership. In 1971 we founded our State Public Affairs Committee (SPAC) to develop and promote legislation benefiting women and children. Later in the decade, we established the Chinatown After-School and Burn Prevention Education programs. In 1976 members launched the JLSF's first Cookbook Committee, ultimately publishing its first cookbook, *San Francisco à la Carte*, in 1979. The widely anticipated collection of distinctively multicultural San Francisco recipes generated impressive pre-sales of 30,000 copies. *San Francisco à la Carte* ranked atop the local bestseller list for several weeks and received a prestigious Best Cookbook Tastemaker award.

San Francisco á la Carte included a recipe for one of San Francisco's characteristic culinary dishes, Cioppino. The introduction of the hearty, tomato-based fish stew to San Francisco has been traced back to Gold Rush days when immigrant Italian fishermen likely brought similar fish dishes from their native Genoa. As for the stew's name—some think it comes from Italy, while others think it derives from the local fishermen's practice of asking one another to "chip in-o" more seafood to the bubbling pot. You can still find delicious Cioppino in the north end of San Francisco at Fishermen's Wharf, which began as a sardine canning center in the 1860s. The area further developed over the next one hundred years to include a full-scale seafood market including fish, crab, and oyster wholesalers along with restaurants catering to tourists. The campaign to restore an aging Fisherman's Wharf began in the mid-70s and was later completed by Mayor Dianne Feinstein in the mid-80s.

As the gay rights movement grew in the Castro neighborhood, under the aegis of photographer-turned-grassroots organizer Harvey Milk, the food movement also continued to grow. In 1972—finding a receptive Bay Area audience for her pioneering food philosophy—Alice Waters opened Chez Panisse in a converted Berkeley apartment building, revolutionizing the Bay Area palate and foodshed. Sourcing the best quality fresh local ingredients, Waters created a California cuisine based on regional provisioning and French culinary techniques.

1971–1980

CALIFORNIA CIOPPINO

A San Francisco staple and popular dish best served with
Boudin Bakery sourdough bread.

SERVES 8

2 (1 1/2- to 2-pound) Dungeness
   crabs, cooked
24 small to medium clams, scrubbed
1 cup dry white wine
1/3 cup olive oil
3 large garlic cloves, minced
1 onion, finely chopped
1 green bell pepper,
   coarsely chopped
2 pounds fresh tomatoes, peeled,
   seeded and chopped
3 tablespoons tomato paste

2 cups dry white wine
1 tablespoon finely chopped fresh
   basil, or 1/2 teaspoon dried basil
1/2 teaspoon dried oregano
1 teaspoon freshly ground pepper
2 pounds fresh fish, such as
   sea bass, rock cod or halibut,
   cut into large pieces
12 ounces scallops
12 ounces uncooked shrimp, peeled
   and deveined
Chopped fresh parsley, for garnish

Special Equipment: *fine-mesh sieve, cheesecloth*

Remove the legs and claws from the crabs and break the bodies into halves, reserving as much of the soft mustard-colored centers, known as crab butter, as possible. Reserve the pieces and press the crab butter through a fine-mesh sieve into a small bowl. Combine the clams with 1 cup white wine in a saucepan. Cover and steam over medium heat for 4 to 6 minutes or until the clams open. Remove the clams, discarding any that do not open. Strain the cooking liquid through a cheesecloth into a bowl. Reserve the clams and cooking liquid.

Heat the olive oil in an 8-quart stockpot over medium heat. Add the garlic, onion, and bell pepper and sauté for 5 minutes or just until the vegetables are tender. Stir in the tomatoes, tomato paste, 2 cups white wine, the reserved cooking liquid, basil, oregano and pepper. Simmer, loosely covered, for 20 minutes.

Add the fish, scallops, shrimp, crabs and crab butter. Simmer for 5 minutes or until the seafood is cooked through; do not stir. Add the clams and cook for just 1 minute. Garnish with parsley and serve immediately.

Dungeness Crab Lettuce Cups

PAIRS WELL WITH
GLORIA FERRER BLANC DE NOIRS

SERVES 6

Lime Fish Sauce
Juice of 2 limes
2 tablespoons fish sauce
1 teaspoon minced serrano chile (seeds optional)
1/2 teaspoon light brown sugar
3 tablespoons extra-virgin olive oil

Lettuce Cups
12 ounces fresh Dungeness crab meat, cooked,
*   cleaned and chopped*
1 avocado, chopped
3/4 cup chopped mango
6 mint leaves, chiffonade
2 tablespoons finely chopped cilantro
2 tablespoons finely chopped shallots
1 tablespoon finely chopped fresh ginger
Small inside leaves of 2 heads Bibb lettuce, iceberg lettuce
*   or butter lettuce*

Sauce
Combine the lime juice, fish sauce, chile and brown sugar in a small bowl; mix well. Whisk in the olive oil.

Lettuce Cups
Combine the crab meat with the avocado, mango, mint, cilantro, shallots and ginger in a medium bowl. Add the lime fish sauce and toss to mix well. Spoon the crab mixture into the lettuce cups and serve immediately.

Pacific Crab Cakes

PAIRS WELL WITH
FAR NIENTE ESTATE BOTTLED CHARDONNAY

SERVES 8

2 eggs, beaten
1/2 cup mayonnaise
1 teaspoon Worcestershire sauce
1 small red bell pepper, very finely chopped
1/2 cup butter cracker crumbs
1/4 cup bread crumbs
2 tablespoons chopped chives
2 tablespoons chopped parsley
1/2 teaspoon red pepper flakes (optional)
1/2 teaspoon each salt and pepper
1 to 1 1/4 pounds Dungeness crab meat, cooked,
*   cleaned and coarsely chopped*
1/2 cup olive oil
Lemon juice for drizzling
Chopped parsley and lemon wedges, for garnish

Combine the eggs, mayonnaise and Worcestershire sauce in a large bowl and mix well. Add the bell pepper, cracker crumbs, bread crumbs, chives, 2 tablespoons parsley, the red pepper flakes, salt and pepper; mix well. Add the crab meat, mixing gently to preserve larger pieces. Shape into eight cakes. Cover and chill in the refrigerator for 1 to 24 hours.

Let the crab cakes stand at room temperature for 1 hour. Heat the olive oil in a large nonstick skillet over medium-high heat. Add the crab cakes and fry for 3 minutes on each side; do not overcook to avoid a thick crust. Drizzle with lemon juice and garnish with additional parsley and lemon wedges.

SEARED SCALLOPS WITH APPLE-BRANDY CREAM SAUCE

PAIRS WELL WITH SÉMILLON

SERVES 8

1/2 tablespoon extra-virgin olive oil
1 large shallot, minced
1/3 cup brandy
1 cup heavy cream
16 large sea scallops, patted dry
Salt and fresh ground pepper to taste
1/2 tablespoon vegetable oil
1/2 cup fresh unfiltered apple juice
1 teaspoon chopped fresh thyme
1 tablespoon extra-virgin olive oil
1 large garlic clove, minced
9 ounces fresh spinach leaves

Preheat the oven to 300 degrees. Heat 1/2 tablespoon olive oil in a large nonstick skillet over medium-high heat. Add the shallot and sauté for 30 seconds. Remove from the heat and add the brandy. Return to the heat and cook for 30 seconds. Stir in the cream and cook for 2 minutes longer for the sauce base. Remove to a bowl. You can prepare the sauce base in advance and let stand at room temperature for up to 2 hours.

Season the scallops with salt and pepper. Heat the vegetable oil in a large nonstick skillet over high heat. Add the scallops half at a time and cook for 2 minutes on each side or until brown. Remove to a rimmed baking sheet and place in the oven to keep warm.

Add the apple juice and thyme to the hot skillet. Cook for 1 minute, stirring up the browned bits from the bottom of the skillet. Add the sauce base and bring to a boil.

Heat 1 tablespoon olive oil in a large saucepan over medium-high heat. Add the garlic and sauté for 30 seconds. Stir in the spinach and sauté for 2 minutes or until it begins to wilt but is still bright green, tossing to cook evenly. Season with salt and pepper. Mound on eight serving plates using tongs. Top each with two scallops.

Stir any juices remaining on the baking sheet into the cream sauce in the skillet. Cook for 2 minutes or until thickened. Season with salt and pepper and spoon over the scallops.

CHEF'S TIP: Fresh, unfiltered apple juice is thicker and has a more intense flavor than regular bottled apple juice. Look for it in the produce section, on ice, or in the refrigerated section at your grocery store.

THIS PAGE GRACIOUSLY SPONSORED BY DARIANA & MASON ROSS

SHRIMP AND BUTTERNUT SQUASH RISOTTO

This is a wonderful fall dish, but butternut squash can be found any time of the year.

PAIRS WELL WITH DRY RIESLING

SERVES 4

3 to 5 cups vegetable stock or fish stock
2 tablespoons extra-virgin olive oil
2 tablespoons butter
6 shallots, chopped
1 pound butternut squash, peeled, seeded and
    cut into $1/2$-inch pieces
2 garlic cloves, crushed
12 ounces arborio rice
$1/2$ cup dry white wine
8 ounces large shrimp, peeled, deveined and sliced
Salt and freshly ground pepper to taste
2 tablespoons butter
5 tablespoons chopped fresh flat-leaf parsley
4 ounces Parmesan cheese, grated

Bring the stock to a simmer in a saucepan; keep hot. Heat the olive oil with 2 tablespoons butter in a Dutch oven or large heavy saucepan over medium heat. Add the shallots and sauté for 5 minutes or until tender. Add the squash and garlic and sauté for 8 minutes or just until the squash is tender but still firm.

Stir in the rice, coating well. Stir in the wine and cook for 2 minutes or until the wine is absorbed, stirring frequently. Add $1/3$ cup of the heated stock and cook over medium heat for 3 to 5 minutes or until the stock has been absorbed, stirring constantly. Add the shrimp and season with salt and pepper.

Add the desired amount of the remaining stock $1/3$ cup at a time, cooking until the stock is absorbed after each addition and the rice and squash are tender; the process should take about 18 minutes. Stir in 2 tablespoons butter, the parsley and cheese. Serve immediately.

CHEF'S TIP: Shape leftover risotto into small balls to make a delicious appetizer. Dip the balls in lightly beaten egg white and coat with panko. Fry in vegetable oil heated to 375 degrees until crisp.

Seafood and Cheese

Some believe there is a culinary rule that you should not top seafood with cheese. Some chefs are comfortable straying from this rule, however. One such exception is risotto, which is often finished with Parmesan cheese. Testers of this dish agreed, giving it high marks.

SHRIMP JAMBALAYA

SERVES 4

6 ounces andouille sausage, cut into ¼-inch pieces
I tablespoon olive oil
I onion, chopped
3 ribs celery, chopped
2 garlic cloves, minced
I green bell pepper, chopped
2 teaspoons paprika
I cup white rice
I (28-ounce) can plum tomatoes, chopped
3 cups water
I pound shrimp, peeled and deveined
Salt and freshly ground pepper to taste
½ cup chopped green onions, for garnish

Sauté the sausage in the olive oil in a large saucepan over medium-high heat for 3 to 4 minutes. Add the onion and sauté until translucent. Add the celery, garlic, bell pepper and paprika; sauté for 3 to 4 minutes longer.

Stir in the rice, undrained tomatoes and water; mix well. Reduce the heat and simmer, covered, for 15 minutes. Add the shrimp and simmer for 5 minutes longer or until the shrimp are pink and the rice is tender. Season with salt and pepper. Ladle into bowls and garnish with the green onions.

HALIBUT IN CRAZY WATER

Courtesy of Chef Sean Baker, Gather

SERVES 2

¼ cup extra-virgin olive oil
3 shallots, sliced
½ fennel bulb, thinly sliced
2 Calabrian chiles or other hot Italian chiles, thinly sliced
2 garlic cloves, thinly sliced
3 tablespoons tomato paste
I teaspoon ground cumin
I teaspoon ground coriander
I cup light dry white wine
½ cup fresh seawater or salted tap water
I pound halibut, cut into I-inch pieces
Chopped leaves of ¼ bunch flat-leaf parsley
I tablespoon chopped fresh oregano
High-quality olive oil for drizzling

Heat a large heavy skillet over medium heat. Add ¼ cup olive oil and heat until smoking. Add the shallots, fennel, chiles and garlic. Sauté for 4 minutes or until tender and lightly caramelized. Stir in the tomato paste, cumin and coriander; sauté for I minute longer. Add the wine and cook for 2 minutes or until the alcohol has evaporated.

Add the seawater and reduce the heat to low. Simmer for 6 minutes to blend the flavors. Add the halibut and cook for 2 minutes or until the fish flakes easily. Stir in the parsley and oregano. Serve in a shallow bowl and drizzle with additional olive oil.

FISH TACOS WITH TOMATO-MANGO SALSA

PAIRS WELL WITH DANE CELLARS DRY CHENIN BLANC, CLARKSBURG

SERVES 4

Tomato-Mango Salsa

4 tomatoes, seeded and chopped
2 mangoes, cut into cubes (see below)
4 garlic cloves, minced
1 jalapeño chile, seeded and minced
1/2 cup chopped fresh cilantro
1/4 cup chopped red onion
Juice of 2 limes
2 to 3 tablespoons olive oil
1 teaspoon salt

Fish Tacos

1 teaspoon ground cumin
1 teaspoon cinnamon
1 teaspoon garlic powder
1 teaspoon onion powder
1 1/2 teaspoons salt
1/4 teaspoon cayenne pepper
1 pound skinless firm white fish, such as
    snapper or tilapia
Juice of 2 limes
1/4 cup Mexican beer
1 teaspoon canola oil
Lime juice to taste
Salt and freshly ground pepper to taste
8 corn tortillas

Salsa

Combine the tomatoes, mangoes, garlic, jalapeño chile and cilantro in a bowl. Add the onion, lime juice, olive oil and salt; mix well. Cover and chill in the refrigerator for 1 hour.

Tacos

Mix the cumin, cinnamon, garlic powder, onion powder, salt and cayenne pepper in a small bowl. Sprinkle over both sides of the fish and place in a glass dish. Add the juice of two limes and the beer. Cover and marinate in the refrigerator for 1 hour.

Heat the canola oil in a heavy saucepan over medium-high heat. Add the fish and marinade to the saucepan and simmer until the fish flakes easily, stirring to break the fish into smaller pieces; drain. Spoon into a serving dish and sprinkle with additional lime juice, salt and pepper. Serve with the corn tortillas and the salsa.

How to Porcupine a Mango

Cut the mango down either side of the large flat seed to form two halves; remove the seed. Score the mango into squares, cutting to but not through the skin. Push up the skin of the mango to invert the mango and lift the squares; cut along the skin to remove the squares.

Greek Sea Bass in Parchment Paper

SERVES 4

5 ounces fresh baby spinach
8 fresh basil leaves
1 (7-ounce) jar roasted red peppers, drained and sliced
20 kalamata olives, pitted and cut into halves
1/2 small red onion, thinly sliced
Dried basil, salt and pepper to taste
Juice of 2 lemons
2 tablespoons butter, melted
4 (6-ounce) skinless sea bass fillets

Preheat the oven to 375 degrees. Cut four pieces of baking parchment about the size of placemats. Mound the spinach in the center of each parchment piece and top each with two basil leaves. Add the roasted red peppers, olives and onion.

Sprinkle both sides of the fish with dried basil, salt and pepper. Place over the layers on the baking parchment and drizzle with the lemon juice and butter. Fold in the sides of the parchment and crease to seal; roll and seal the top and bottom to enclose completely and retain the flavors while cooking.

Place on a baking sheet and bake for 15 minutes. Serve in the baking parchment, allowing guests to open the packets at the table with caution to watch for steam.

THIS PAGE GRACIOUSLY SPONSORED BY LESLIE KARREN

Plank-Grilled Salmon with Brown Sugar Glaze

Grilling planks add a wonderful smoky flavor to dishes, even on a gas grill.
Choose maple, cedar, alder, or other appropriate wood.

SERVES 4

1 tablespoon dry mustard
2 tablespoons soy sauce
1 tablespoon brown sugar
1 pound salmon, skin on and pin bones removed

Special Equipment: *wood grilling plank*

Soak a wood grilling plank in water for 2 hours or longer. Mix the dry mustard with enough of the soy sauce to form a paste in a small bowl. Mix in the remaining soy sauce and the brown sugar. Spread half over the salmon and marinate for 30 minutes.

Heat a grill until hot. Remove the plank from the water and place the salmon skin side down on the plank. Place on the grill over indirect heat. Drizzle half the remaining glaze over the salmon.

Grill for 10 to 15 minutes and then drizzle with the remaining glaze. Grill for 5 minutes longer or until the salmon flakes easily. Serve on the plank, if desired.

CHEF'S TIP: For indirect grilling, heat the grill using all burners. Turn off all but one of the burners when ready to grill and place the food away from the active burner to grill.

THIS PAGE GRACIOUSLY SPONSORED BY SARA & PAUL BORZCIK

LEMON DIJON-CRUSTED SALMON

PAIRS WELL WITH SAMUEL ADAMS SUMMER ALE

SERVES 2 TO 3

3/4 cup bread crumbs
1/2 shallot, finely chopped
1/2 cup (1 stick) butter, melted
Juice of 1/2 lemon
2 teaspoons Dijon mustard
1 tablespoon honey
1/2 teaspoon salt
1 (1-pound) boneless skinless salmon fillet
2 tablespoons olive oil
Salt and pepper to taste
Cooked multigrain rice or sautéed greens
Lemon wedges and parsley sprigs, for garnish

Preheat the oven to 375 degrees. Combine the bread crumbs and shallot in a small bowl. Add the butter, lemon juice, Dijon mustard, honey and 1/2 teaspoon salt and mix to form a thick paste. Place the salmon in a medium baking dish and drizzle with the olive oil; season lightly with salt and pepper. Press the bread crumb mixture over the fish. Bake for 20 minutes.

Set the oven to broil and broil the fish for 2 minutes to brown. Serve on a bed of multigrain rice or sautéed greens and garnish with lemon wedges and parsley.

GRILLED FISH WITH LEMON CAPER SAUCE

PAIRS WELL WITH CADE SAUVIGNON BLANC

SERVES 6

1/2 cup sour cream
1/4 cup mayonnaise
1 tablespoon lemon juice
1 teaspoon chopped fresh dill weed
Salt to taste
1/2 teaspoon freshly ground pepper
1 tablespoon minced onion
1 tablespoon chopped capers
3 pounds fish

Combine the sour cream, mayonnaise, lemon juice, dill weed, salt, pepper, onion and capers in a bowl and mix well. Grill the fish as desired. Serve with the sauce.

Swordfish Caponata

PAIRS WELL WITH MAZZOCCO SONOMA STUHLMULLER RESERVE CHARDONNAY

SERVES 4

Caponata

1/2 cup olive oil
1 large eggplant, cut into 1/2-inch pieces
2 tablespoons all-purpose flour
Salt and freshly ground pepper to taste
1/4 cup olive oil
2 red onions, finely chopped
2 zucchini, finely chopped
2 celery ribs, finely chopped
2 cups sweet cherry tomatoes
1 (3-ounce) jar mixed pitted olives, drained
1/4 cup capers, drained
1/4 cup red wine vinegar
1 tablespoon brown sugar

Swordfish

4 (6-ounce) swordfish steaks
2 tablespoons butter, melted
Juice of 1 lemon
4 sprigs of rosemary, for garnish

Caponata

Heat 1/2 cup olive oil in a large skillet. Coat the eggplant with the flour, salt and pepper. Add to the skillet in batches and sauté for 8 minutes or until tender and brown. Drain on paper towels.

Wipe the skillet lightly and add 1/4 cup olive oil. Add the onions and sauté until tender. Add the zucchini and celery and sauté for 5 minutes. Return the eggplant to the skillet and add the tomatoes, olives, capers, red wine vinegar and brown sugar. Simmer for 10 minutes or until the vegetables are tender. Adjust the seasonings and keep warm over low heat, stirring occasionally.

Swordfish

Preheat the grill. Brush the swordfish lightly with the butter and lemon juice. Place on the grill and grill for 5 to 10 minutes on each side or until the fish flakes easily, brushing with the remaining butter and lemon juice as it cooks.

Spoon some of the caponata onto serving plates and add the swordfish steaks; top with the remaining caponata and garnish with the rosemary sprigs.

THIS PAGE GRACIOUSLY SPONSORED BY SHANNON MURPHY & THE MURPHY FAMILY

Poultry

During the 1980s, the JLSF celebrated our seventy-fifth anniversary and co-hosted the sixtieth AJLI Annual Conference. As social crises reached epidemic proportions, the JLSF worked diligently to address critical issues like homelessness, child care, education of disadvantaged youth, substance abuse, and HIV/AIDS. At the very end of the decade, the JLSF provided critical support in the aftermath of the 7.0 Loma Prieta earthquake, which shocked the Bay Area on October 17, 1989. In the days immediately following the earthquake, the JLSF established a volunteer needs bank and provided clothing from the Next-to-New Shop to those left homeless by the disaster.

On the culinary front, in 1987 the JLSF followed their successful *San Francisco à la Carte* with its second cookbook, *San Francisco Encore*, which emphasized the fresh local cuisine characteristic of Bay Area food culture. Established in Hayes Valley in 1979, and now run by Chez Panisse alumna Judy Rodgers, Zuni Café is famous for its emphasis on fresh local food epitomized by its roasted chicken with arugula and bread salad. No ordinary roasted chicken, Rodgers' coveted recipe has diners patiently waiting for the hour it takes to prepare. Before Rodgers' roasted chicken, Chicken Tetrazzini was San Francisco's most famous chicken recipe, created by the Palace Hotel in honor of Italian opera star Luisa Tetrazzini and her 1910 Christmas Eve performance. The decadent dish's ingredients include chicken, sherry, cream, pasta, and Parmesan cheese.

Inspired by the ore-hauling carts of the Gold Rush era, San Francisco's iconic cable cars originated in the 1870s with the Clay Street Hill Railroad. By the 1980s, the system had fallen into serious disrepair. Between 1982 and 1984, the city undertook major efforts to restore the transportation network to its former grandeur. As a result of the reconstructive effort, the Hyde Street cable car line now extends to the turnaround at Beach Street in Fishermen's Wharf. One block away is Ghirardelli Square, which was granted National Historic Register status in 1982. Once a chocolate factory, Ghiradelli Square is now home to several shops and restaurants.

1981–1990

CHICKEN WITH KALAMATA OLIVES AND LEMON

SERVES 6 TO 8

3 pounds boneless skinless
    chicken breasts and thighs
Salt and freshly ground
    black pepper to taste
1/4 cup olive oil
1 large yellow onion,
    thinly sliced
6 garlic cloves, crushed
2 teaspoons turmeric
1 teaspoon ground cumin

1 teaspoon coriander
Pinch of red pepper flakes
1 cup chicken broth
Juice and grated zest of
    2 lemons
1 cup pitted kalamata olives
1 bay leaf
1 cinnamon stick
2 tablespoons chopped fresh
    mint, for garnish

Preheat the oven to 350 degrees. Season the chicken with salt and black pepper. Heat 2 tablespoons of the olive oil in a large skillet over medium-high heat. Add the chicken in batches and fry for 4 to 5 minutes on each side, adding the remaining 2 tablespoons olive oil as needed. Remove to a deep baking dish or Dutch oven using a slotted spoon. Add the onion and garlic to the drippings in the skillet and sauté over medium-high heat for 10 minutes or until golden brown. Stir in the turmeric, cumin, coriander and red pepper flakes. Cook for 1 to 2 minutes. Add the broth, 1/4 cup of the lemon juice and the lemon zest and cook for 3 minutes.

Spoon over the chicken and add the olives, bay leaf and cinnamon stick. Bake, covered, for 20 minutes. Uncover and bake for 20 minutes longer or until the liquid is reduced to the desired consistency. Discard the bay leaf and cinnamon stick; season with salt and pepper. Drizzle with the remaining lemon juice and garnish with the mint. Serve with white or wild rice and grilled vegetables.

CHEF'S TIP: Serve leftover chicken cold over a green salad. This recipe is also delicious using bone-in meat.

LEMON CHICKEN WITH ARTICHOKE HEARTS

PAIRS WELL WITH MA(I)SONRY NAPA VALLEY SAUVIGNON BLANC

SERVES 4

4 boneless skinless chicken breasts
1/2 cup all-purpose flour
1 teaspoon salt
1/2 teaspoon pepper
1/4 cup olive oil
2 tablespoons unsalted butter, melted
1/2 cup dry white wine
1 (12-ounce) can whole artichoke hearts in water, drained
    and cut into quarters
2 tablespoons unsalted butter
1/4 cup fresh lemon juice
2 tablespoons chopped fresh flat-leaf parsley
Hot cooked pasta or couscous, or fresh spinach leaves

Slice the chicken horizontally and pound 1/2 inch thick. Coat with a mixture of the flour, salt and pepper. Heat 2 tablespoons of the olive oil and 2 tablespoons butter in a large skillet over medium-high heat. Add half the chicken at a time and sauté for 2 to 3 minutes on each side or until golden brown, adding the remaining olive oil between batches. Remove to a plate and tent with foil to keep warm. Drain excess drippings from the skillet.

Add the wine to the skillet and cook until reduced by half, stirring up the browned bits from the skillet. Add the artichoke hearts and cook for 30 seconds. Remove from the heat and stir in 2 tablespoons butter, the lemon juice and parsley. Serve the chicken over pasta, couscous or a bed of spinach. Top with the artichokes and sauce.

ROASTED CHICKEN WITH CARROTS, ONIONS AND POTATOES

PAIRS WELL WITH GLORIA FERRER CARNEROS CHARDONNAY

SERVES 4

3 carrots, cut into quarters
2 yellow onions, cut into quarters
8 ounces small roasting potatoes, cut into quarters
1 (4- to 5-pound) whole roasting chicken
Salt and freshly ground pepper to taste
1 lemon, cut into halves
Cloves of 1 head garlic
1 bunch of fresh thyme
1/2 cup (1 stick) butter, melted

Preheat the oven to 425 degrees. Place the carrots, onions and potatoes in a roasting pan. Rinse the chicken inside and out; remove any giblets and pat the chicken dry with paper towels. Sprinkle inside and out with salt and pepper. Stuff half the lemon, the garlic and thyme into the chicken cavity; close the cavity opening with the remaining lemon half. Place in the roasting pan, tucking the vegetables under the chicken.

Brush the butter on the chicken with a pastry brush. Roast the chicken for 18 minutes per pound or until the skin is brown and the juices run clear, brushing with butter every 15 minutes. Let stand for 10 minutes before carving. Serve with the roasted vegetables.

CHEF'S TIP: This recipe is very flexible. You can substitute a lime or orange for the lemon. You can use other fresh herbs, choosing a combination of two or three herbs that you enjoy. Feel free to experiment to find the herb blend that you like, or to substitute dried herbs for the fresh herbs.

THIS PAGE GRACIOUSLY SPONSORED BY COURTNEY & NICK BOCCI

CHICKEN STUFFED WITH CARAMELIZED ONIONS AND GOAT CHEESE

PAIRS WELL WITH SAMUEL ADAMS BOSTON LAGER

SERVES 6

1 1/2 tablespoons olive oil

1 1/3 cups thinly sliced white or yellow onions,
    about 1 pound

1/4 teaspoon salt

1/4 teaspoon freshly ground pepper

3/4 cup (3 ounces) grated or shredded Parmesan cheese

2 ounces goat cheese

1 tablespoon chopped fresh flat-leaf parsley

1 tablespoon milk

1 1/2 teaspoons chopped fresh thyme

1/4 teaspoon salt

6 boneless skinless chicken thighs (about 2 1/4 pounds)

1/4 teaspoon salt

1/2 cup dry white wine

1 cup chicken broth

Heat the olive oil in a large skillet over medium heat. Add the onions, 1/4 teaspoon salt and the pepper; sauté for 12 minutes. Cover and reduce the heat. Cook for 8 minutes, stirring occasionally. Uncover and cook for 5 minutes longer, stirring occasionally. Cool slightly. Combine with the Parmesan cheese, goat cheese, parsley, milk, thyme and 1/4 teaspoon salt in a small bowl; mix with a fork.

Pound the chicken 1/4 inch thick between sheets of baking parchment. Place 1 1/2 tablespoons of the cheese mixture in the center of each piece of chicken and roll to enclose the filling; secure each with two wooden picks. Sprinkle evenly with 1/4 teaspoon salt.

Heat a skillet sprayed with nonstick cooking spray over medium-high heat. Add the chicken and sauté for 5 minutes. Turn the chicken and reduce the heat. Cook, covered, for 10 minutes longer or until cooked through. Remove to a serving plate and let stand for 10 minutes.

Add the white wine to the skillet and bring to a boil over medium-high heat, scraping to loosen the browned bits from the skillet. Cook for 2 minutes or until reduced by half. Add the broth and cook for 9 minutes or until reduced to 1/4 cup. Serve with the chicken.

CHEF'S TIP: A mallet or the bottom of an iron skillet or heavy saucepan can be used to pound the chicken.

Chicken Provençal

Great for a weeknight dinner party or large crowd, as it should be made the day before.

SERVES 10 TO 12

1 1/2 cups white mushrooms, sliced
1/3 cup oil-pack sun-dried tomatoes, chopped
1/3 cup capers, drained
1/4 cup minced garlic
1/4 cup olive oil
3 tablespoons white wine vinegar
2 tablespoons dried thyme
1 1/2 tablespoons dried rosemary
2 teaspoons sugar
1 1/2 teaspoons salt
1/2 teaspoon freshly ground pepper
6 pounds boneless skinless chicken breasts, cut into quarters
1/2 cup white wine
1/2 cup fine bread crumbs
1/2 cup (2 ounces) grated Parmesan cheese
Parsley, for garnish

Combine the mushrooms, sun-dried tomatoes, capers, garlic, olive oil, white wine vinegar, thyme, rosemary, sugar, salt and pepper in a 9×13-inch baking dish; mix well. Add the chicken and turn to coat evenly. Cover with plastic wrap and marinate in the refrigerator for 12 hours or longer.

Preheat the oven to 350 degrees. Pour the wine over the chicken and cover with foil. Bake for 10 minutes. Baste with the pan juices and bake, uncovered, for 10 minutes; baste again. Mix the bread crumbs and cheese in a small bowl. Sprinkle over the chicken. Bake for 30 minutes, basting after 15 minutes. Garnish with parsley and serve warm with couscous.

Sweet Curried Mustard Chicken

PAIRS WELL WITH GLORIA FERRER CARNEROS CHARDONNAY

SERVES 4

4 boneless skinless chicken breasts
1/2 cup (2 ounces) grated Parmesan cheese
1/2 cup honey
1/4 cup Dijon mustard
3 tablespoons butter, melted
1 tablespoon curry powder
1/2 teaspoon salt
1/4 teaspoon freshly ground pepper

Arrange the chicken in a 9×13-inch baking dish. Combine the cheese, honey, Dijon mustard, butter, curry powder, salt and pepper in a bowl and mix well. Spoon evenly over the chicken. Bake for 1 hour or until golden brown, basting with the pan juices every 15 minutes.

CHEF'S TIP: For a spicier version, substitute cayenne pepper for the curry powder. For extra crunch, sprinkle the top with a mixture of Parmesan cheese and bread crumbs.

Tarragon and Mustard Chicken

PAIRS WELL WITH SAMUEL ADAMS LIGHT OR GLORIA FERRER CARNEROS CHARDONNAY

SERVES 4

4 boneless skinless chicken breasts
Salt and freshly ground pepper to taste
2 tablespoons clarified butter
1/4 cup finely chopped shallots
1/4 cup dry white wine
2 tablespoons whole grain Dijon mustard
1/2 cup heavy cream
3 tablespoons chopped fresh tarragon

Season the chicken with salt and pepper. Heat the clarified butter in a sauté pan over medium-high heat. Add the chicken and sauté for 5 minutes on each side or until brown and cooked through. Remove to a platter and tent with foil to keep warm.

Add the shallots to the drippings in the skillet and sauté for 2 minutes. Add the wine and Dijon mustard and bring to a simmer. Add the cream and 2 tablespoons of the tarragon. Simmer for 3 minutes or until slightly thickened, stirring frequently. Return the chicken and any accumulated juices to the skillet. Cook just until heated through.

Place the chicken on a serving plate and top with the sauce. Sprinkle with the remaining 1 tablespoon tarragon. Serve with steamed green beans.

Clarified Butter

To clarify butter, melt butter in a small saucepan over low heat until the fat solids begin to separate. Skim off the foam that rises to the top. The clear butter that remains in the saucepan is clarified butter.

THIS PAGE GRACIOUSLY SPONSORED BY SUZY PAK & MARK GUNDACKER

HOISIN STIR-FRIED CHICKEN

PAIRS WELL WITH GLORIA FERRER VA DE VI

SERVES 4

1 egg white
1 1/2 tablespoons cornstarch
3/4 teaspoon salt
4 boneless skinless chicken breasts, cut into 1-inch pieces
1/4 cup peanut oil
4 green onions, chopped
2 tablespoons hoisin sauce
3/4 tablespoon soy sauce

Whisk the egg white with the cornstarch and salt in a bowl. Add the chicken and toss to coat evenly. Heat the peanut oil in a large saucepan or wok over medium-high heat until very hot. Add the chicken and sauté for 3 minutes or until brown. Remove the chicken to a bowl; reserve 2 tablespoons of the peanut oil in the saucepan.

Heat the peanut oil and add the green onions. Sauté for 2 to 3 minutes. Return the chicken to the saucepan and stir in the hoisin sauce and soy sauce. Cook for 10 minutes or until the chicken is cooked through. Serve with fresh Asian noodles or rice.

SPICED BUTTERFLIED QUAIL

Courtesy of Chef Gerald Hirigoyen, Piperade

PAIRS WELL WITH CADE ESTATE
CABERNET SAUVIGNON

SERVES 4

1 teaspoon coriander seeds
Seeds of 3 cardamom pods
1 teaspoon black peppercorns
2 garlic cloves, thinly sliced
1 large shallot, thinly sliced
Grated zest of 1 small orange
1/4 cup extra-virgin olive oil
1 tablespoon dark
    brown sugar
1/4 teaspoon ground
    cinnamon
Pinch each of ground mace
    and ground cloves
4 quails, deboned and
    wings removed
Fleur de sel or coarse salt
    to taste

Special Equipment: *mortar and pestle*

Combine the coriander seeds, cardamom seeds and peppercorns in a mortar and crush to a coarse powder with a pestle. You can also use the bottom edge of a heavy saucepan to crush the spices. Combine with the garlic, shallot, orange zest, olive oil, brown sugar, cinnamon, mace and cloves in a small bowl; mix well.

Split the quail down the backs and butterfly on a work surface. Rub the spice mixture over the entire surface. Marinate, covered, in the refrigerator for 4 to 12 hours.

Heat a griddle, cast-iron skillet or sauté pan over high heat until very hot. Decrease the heat to medium-high and add the quail skin side down. Sauté for 4 minutes or until brown. Turn the quail with tongs and cook for 4 minutes longer or until brown. Remove to a warmed serving platter and sprinkle with fleur de sel.

ROASTED TURKEY WITH CRANBERRY MERLOT SAUCE

PAIRS WELL WITH BLACKBIRD VINEYARDS
CONTRARIAN PROPRIETARY RED WINE

SERVES 8

$^1/4$ cup merlot
$^1/4$ cup fresh orange juice
$^1/2$ cup water
$^3/4$ cup granulated sugar
$^1/4$ cup packed light brown sugar
12 ounces fresh cranberries
$^1/2$ teaspoon grated orange zest
1 teaspoon grated lemon zest
1 (12-pound) roasted turkey

Blend the wine, orange juice and water in a large saucepan. Add the granulated sugar and brown sugar and mix well. Heat over medium-high heat, stirring to dissolve the sugars completely. Add the cranberries. Reduce the heat and simmer for 10 to 12 minutes or until the cranberries pop, stirring occasionally. Stir in the orange zest and lemon zest. Cool slightly and serve over the roasted turkey.

TURKEY CHILI

PAIRS WELL WITH ROSATI FAMILY WINERY
CABERNET SAUVIGNON, MENDICINO COUNTY

SERVES 8

2 tablespoons vegetable oil
   or corn oil
2 white or yellow onions,
   chopped (about 2 cups)
1 red bell pepper, chopped
6 garlic cloves, minced
   (about 2 tablespoons)
2 to 4 tablespoons chili
   powder, or more to taste
1 tablespoon ground cumin
2 teaspoons ground coriander
1 teaspoon dried oregano
$^1/2$ to 1 teaspoon red pepper
   flakes, or to taste
$^1/4$ to $^1/2$ teaspoon cayenne
   pepper, or to taste

2 pounds (93% lean)
   ground turkey
2 (15-ounce) cans dark red
   kidney beans, drained
   and rinsed
1 (28-ounce) can each
   diced tomatoes and
   crushed tomatoes
2 cups low-sodium
   chicken broth
1 teaspoon kosher salt
Black pepper to taste
Lime wedges, sour cream,
   chopped cilantro,
   shredded cheese and
   tortilla chips, for topping

Heat the oil in a large Dutch oven over medium heat. Add the onions, bell pepper, garlic, chili powder, coriander, cumin, oregano, red pepper flakes and cayenne pepper. Sauté until the vegetables are tender and start to brown. Increase the heat to medium-high and add half the turkey, Sauté just until it begins to brown, stirring with a wooden spoon to crumble.

Add the beans, diced tomatoes, crushed tomatoes, broth and kosher salt. Bring to a boil. Reduce the heat and simmer for 1 hour, stirring occasionally. Shape the remaining turkey into small balls. Stir into the chili. Simmer for 40 minutes, stirring occasionally and adding water or chicken broth if needed for the desired consistency. Season with black pepper. Adjust the chili powder and salt. Serve with the desired toppings.

Meats

The 1990s proved to be an amazingly active decade for the JLSF, which concentrated considerable efforts toward health and domestic violence initiatives. At the beginning of the decade, the JLSF co-sponsored a dinner with the San Francisco AIDS Foundation at the International AIDS Conference and held its first open Community Forum on Breast Cancer. In 1996, to support the National Silent Witness Initiative against domestic violence, the JLSF constructed Silent Witness silhouettes and exhibited them around the Bay Area. Its efforts to this cause culminated in a march against domestic violence in Washington, D.C., the following year. Fundraising activities included a rock concert and companion CD, *Mad About Monet*, at the DeYoung Museum, a *Phantom of the Opera* night and the first annual Kitchen Tour. The JLSF's 1992 children's book, *The City by the Bay*, ranked number one on Bay Area children's best-seller lists. As for our famous cookbooks, we released *San Francisco Flavors* in 1999, highlighting a collection of members' cherished recipes and melding international flair with local ingredients.

In the food world, prosperity from San Francisco's technology boom sparked renewed interest in a glamorous steakhouse culture that included notable restaurants like Alfred's and Harris', famous as much for their aged cuts of meat, as for their classic cocktails, private dining rooms, and luxurious service. As interest in healthful lean meats increased, Bill Niman built his namesake Marin County-based Niman Ranch brand to provide high-quality, sustainable meat. Boosted by Chez Panisse's inclusion of his brand on its menu, Niman's beef and pork became widely recognized as the gold standard for gourmet meat. The embrace of principled ranching and meat processing paved the way for artisan-produced salami—now crafted by the likes of Fatted Calf, Incanto, and Boccalone—and for San Francisco's move toward slow and local food in the 2000s.

The refashioning of San Francisco's Hayes Valley neighborhood into a gourmet restaurant destination also took place over the course of the decade. While Zuni Café was the neighborhood's culinary pioneer, restaurants like Jardinière, Absinthe, Citizen Cake, and the Hayes Street Grill, featuring internationally renowned chefs and bartenders, sprang up and flourished. In 1994 Crissy Field, once part of the Presidio military base, transformed into an open-space recreation area where residents now run, bike, and walk their dogs—all along the beautiful San Francisco Bay front with spectacular views of the Golden Gate Bridge.

1991–2000

PANCETTA-STUDDED BEEF TENDERLOIN

PAIRS WELL WITH NICKEL & NICKEL SULLENGER VINEYARD CABERNET SAUVIGNON

SERVES 6 TO 8

Beef

1 (3-pound) beef tenderloin, trimmed and tied,
    at room temperature
2 ounces thinly sliced pancetta, cut into 1/2-inch pieces
2 teaspoons kosher salt
2 teaspoons pepper
2 tablespoons vegetable oil

Wine Sauce

1/4 cup finely chopped shallots
1/2 cup dry red wine
1/4 cup dry marsala
3/4 cup beef or veal demi-glace
2 tablespoons currant jelly
1 1/2 tablespoons unsalted butter, chopped
1/4 teaspoon kosher salt
1/8 teaspoon pepper

Special Equipment: *instant-read thermometer,
    fine mesh sieve*

Beef

Preheat the oven to 425 degrees. Pat the tenderloin dry and cut slits 1/2 inch deep at 1-inch intervals all over the roast; insert one piece of pancetta into each slit. Sprinkle with the kosher salt and pepper. Heat the oil in a 12-inch skillet over high heat until smoking. Sauté the tenderloin in the oil for 5 minutes on each side or until brown. Remove to a small roasting pan, reserving the skillet and drippings for the wine sauce.

Place the roasting pan on the middle oven rack and roast for 25 minutes or to 120 degrees on an instant-read thermometer inserted diagonally 2 inches into the center. Remove to a cutting board and tent loosely with foil; let stand for 25 minutes. The tenderloin will continue to cook as it stands, reaching 130 degrees for medium-rare. You can roast the tenderloin to 170 degrees for well-done if preferred.

Sauce

Heat the reserved skillet and drippings over medium-high heat until hot, but not smoking. Add the shallots and sauté for 2 minutes or until golden brown. Add the red wine and marsala, stirring up the browned bits from the skillet. Cook until reduced by one-third. Stir in the demi-glace and jelly and simmer for 2 minutes, whisking vigorously to mix well.

Whisk in the butter gradually. Remove from the heat and whisk in the salt and pepper. Strain through a fine mesh sieve into a medium bowl. Serve over the sliced tenderloin.

CHEF'S TIP: Demi-glace is available in specialty food shops and supermarkets or can be homemade.

GRILLED SIRLOIN STEAKS WITH CHIMICHURRI SAUCE

Courtesy of Chef Stephen Gibbs, Hands On Gourmet and JLSF Kids in the Kitchen Chef

PAIRS WELL WITH ACORN WINERY/ALEGRIA VINEYARDS SANGIOVESE

SERVES 5

Chimichurri Sauce

3/4 cup chopped fresh flat-leaf parsley
1 1/2 tablespoons dried oregano
2 garlic cloves, minced
1/2 cup plus 2 tablespoons olive oil
2 tablespoons red wine vinegar
Juice of 1/2 lemon
1/2 tablespoon paprika
1 tablespoon water
Salt and freshly ground pepper to taste

Steaks

5 (5-ounce) steaks, about 1 1/4 inches thick
Salt and freshly ground pepper to taste

Special Equipment: *instant-read thermometer*

Sauce

Mix the parsley, oregano, garlic, olive oil, red wine vinegar, lemon juice, paprika and water in a small bowl. Season with salt and pepper and mix well.

Steaks

Preheat the grill. Season the steaks with salt and pepper. Grill over medium heat to 125 degrees on an instant-read thermometer for medium-rare, or to the desired degree of doneness. Remove to a cutting board and let stand for 3 to 4 minutes. Remove to a platter and drizzle generously with the sauce.

THIS PAGE GRACIOUSLY SPONSORED BY USHA BURNS & JOANNE HORNING

Red Wine–Braised Short Ribs

Courtesy of Chef Jesse Mallgren, Madrona Manor

PAIRS WELL WITH SAMUEL ADAMS WINTER LAGER

SERVES 4

Wine Marinade

3 Roma tomatoes, cut into halves
2 yellow onions, cut into quarters
2 carrots, peeled and cut into 1-inch pieces
2 ribs celery, cut into 1-inch pieces
4 garlic cloves, cut into halves
4 sprigs of English thyme
2 bay leaves
1 teaspoon black peppercorns
1 (750-milliliter) bottle syrah

Short Ribs

4 (3-bone) beef short ribs, 1 1/2 inches wide
Salt and freshly ground pepper to taste
1/4 cup canola oil
Veal stock
Freshly grated horseradish to taste

Special Equipment: *stovetop-safe roasting pan, cheesecloth*

Marinade

Combine the tomatoes, onions, carrots, celery, garlic, thyme, bay leaves and peppercorns in a large saucepan. Add the wine and bring to a boil over medium heat. Cool to room temperature.

Ribs

Add the short ribs to the marinade and marinate in the refrigerator for 24 hours. Remove the ribs from the marinade and season with salt and pepper. Remove the vegetables from the marinade and discard. Reserve the marinade.

Preheat the oven to 350 degrees. Heat the canola oil in a large saucepan. Add the ribs in batches and cook until evenly browned, removing to a bowl with a slotted spoon.

Pour the reserved marinade into a stovetop-safe roasting pan and bring to a boil over medium heat on the stovetop. Cook until reduced by half. Reduce the heat to a simmer and return the ribs to the pan; add stock if needed to cover the ribs. Bring to a simmer. Place in the oven and roast for 3 1/2 to 4 hours or until tender.

Remove the ribs to a shallow roasting pan. Strain the cooking liquid through a cheesecloth into a saucepan, discarding the solids. Cook over medium-high heat until reduced by one-third. Season with salt and pepper. Pour over the ribs and chill in the refrigerator for 8 to 12 hours.

Preheat the oven to 350 degrees. Heat the ribs for 10 to 15 minutes or until heated through. Remove carefully from the roasting pan and serve with mashed potatoes or polenta. Spoon some of the cooking liquid over the ribs and sprinkle with horseradish.

Spicy Meatball Sliders

PAIRS WELL WITH DANE CELLARS CABERNET SAUVIGNON, SONOMA VALLEY

132

SERVES 6

Meatballs

12 ounces ground beef

12 ounces spicy Italian pork
 sausage, casings removed
 and sausage crumbled

1/2 cup panko (Japanese
 bread crumbs)

1/2 cup water

6 tablespoons grated
 pecorino Romano cheese

1 egg

1 egg yolk

1/4 cup chopped fresh parsley

1 teaspoon salt

1/2 teaspoon freshly ground
 pepper

1/4 cup vegetable oil

Spicy Sauce

1 cup chopped yellow onion

6 garlic cloves, chopped

1/4 cup packed fresh basil
 leaves, chopped

1 1/2 teaspoons fennel seeds

2 tablespoons olive oil

3 (14-ounce) cans whole
 peeled tomatoes

2 tablespoons butter

1 yellow onion, thinly sliced

Mixed baby greens or
 arugula leaves

18 small soft rolls, split
 horizontally

2 tablespoons chopped
 fresh parsley

2 tablespoons grated
 pecorino Romano cheese

Panko

Panko is Japanese bread crumbs. They tend to be lighter, crunchier, and crisper than Western bread crumbs. Panko can be found in supermarkets and specialty food stores.

Meatballs

Mix the ground beef and sausage with the panko, water, cheese, egg, egg yolk, parsley, salt and pepper in a large bowl. Shape into eighteen 2-inch meatballs. Heat the oil in a large skillet over medium-high heat. Add the meatballs in batches and cook for 4 to 5 minutes or until brown, turning with tongs. Remove to a plate and tent with foil.

Sauce

Pour the drippings from the skillet. Sauté the chopped onion, garlic, basil and fennel seeds in the olive oil in the skillet over medium heat for 5 minutes or until the onion begins to brown. Add the undrained tomatoes and bring to a boil, scraping up the browned bits from the skillet. Reduce the heat to low and cover loosely. Simmer for 30 minutes, stirring occasionally.

Purée the sauce in a food processor or with an immersion blender until nearly smooth. Return to the skillet and add the meatballs. Cover loosely and simmer for 30 minutes or until the meatballs are cooked through, stirring occasionally. Melt the butter in a medium saucepan. Add the sliced onion and sauté for 15 to 20 minutes or until caramelized.

Place the greens on the roll bottoms and add one meatball to each. Drizzle with the sauce and sprinkle with the parsley, cheese and caramelized onion. Top with the roll tops.

CHEF'S TIP: The meatballs and sauce can be made a day in advance and stored, covered, in the refrigerator.

Gyros

Recipe appeared originally in San Francisco Encore, *the second cookbook published by* The Junior League of San Francisco, Inc.

SERVES 4 TO 6

Cucumber Sauce

2 cups sour cream
1 cucumber, peeled, seeded and puréed
1 garlic clove, crushed
2 tablespoons sugar
1/2 teaspoon salt

Gyros

1 pound ground lamb
1 large garlic clove, crushed
2 tablespoons chopped fresh parsley
2 teaspoons lemon juice
1/2 teaspoon dried basil
1/2 teaspoon dried thyme
1/2 teaspoon dried rosemary
1/2 teaspoon salt
1/4 teaspoon dried marjoram
3 pita rounds, cut into halves and warmed
2 tomatoes, chopped
1 white or yellow onion, chopped

Sauce

Combine the sour cream, cucumber, garlic, sugar and salt in a small bowl and mix well.

Gyros

Combine the ground lamb, garlic, parsley, lemon juice, basil, thyme, rosemary, salt and marjoram in a large bowl and mix well. Heat a large skillet over medium heat and add the lamb mixture. Sauté until brown, stirring constantly; drain well.

Spoon the lamb mixture into the pita rounds and top with the tomatoes and onion. Spoon the sauce over the top and serve immediately.

THIS PAGE GRACIOUSLY SPONSORED BY BICHHOPE & CO PHAN

RACK OF LAMB WITH PISTACHIO MINT PESTO

PAIRS WELL WITH GLORIA FERRER CARNEROS PINOT NOIR

SERVES 4

1 cup unsalted pistachios, lightly toasted
1 1/2 cups packed mint leaves (about 2 large bunches)
1 cup packed fresh spinach leaves
1/2 cup (2 ounces) freshly grated Parmesan cheese
2 tablespoons lime juice
1 1/2 teaspoons kosher salt
1/2 teaspoon cayenne pepper
1/4 teaspoon freshly ground white pepper
1 cup olive oil
2 (4-pound) racks of lamb, Frenched (see below)

Special Equipment: *instant-read thermometer*

Frenched Rack of Lamb

Rack of lamb is often the most tender cut and is served with several individual bones protruding from it. This style is known as a "Frenched" rack of lamb. It is achieved by trimming the fat and meat from between the ribs and scraping the bones clean. You can ask the butcher to trim the fat and tail from the lamb racks, leaving only a thin layer of fat, and to "French" the ribs.

Grind the pistachios in a food processor or blender. Add the mint, spinach, cheese, lime juice, kosher salt, cayenne pepper and white pepper. Process to a coarse paste. Add the olive oil gradually, processing constantly to form a smooth paste for the pesto.

Heat a large skillet over medium-high heat until very hot. Add the lamb fat side down and sear for 1 to 2 minutes on each side or until brown but still rare in the center, standing the racks on end with tongs to sear the ends. Cool the lamb to room temperature. Chill in the refrigerator. Let stand at room temperature for 15 minutes.

Preheat the oven to 450 degrees. Spread the pesto generously over the underside of the lamb, leaving the bones uncovered. Invert on a rack in a shallow roasting pan and spread the top with the remaining pesto.

Insert an instant-read thermometer into the thickest portion of the lamb without touching a bone. Roast for 15 minutes or to 120 degrees for rare, 130 degrees for medium and 140 degrees for well-done; the pesto will darken as the lamb roasts. Place on a cutting board and let stand for 5 minutes. Carve into chops and serve with couscous.

CHEF'S TIP: The Pistachio Mint Pesto can also be used with pork chops, leg of lamb, or lamb loin. Cut the loin as for a roulade, spread with the pesto, roll to enclose the pesto, and tie with kitchen twine.

Fennel and Garlic Pork Loin

137

PAIRS WELL WITH SAMUEL ADAMS BOSTON
LAGER OR ROSATI FAMILY WINERY CABERNET
SAUVIGNON, MENDOCINO COUNTY

SERVES 8

1 (5-pound) pork loin
6 garlic cloves
1/3 cup chopped fresh rosemary leaves
2 tablespoons grated lemon zest (about 2 lemons)
2 teaspoons fennel seeds
2 tablespoons olive oil
1 tablespoon coarse Dijon mustard
1 tablespoon kosher salt
1 teaspoon freshly ground pepper

Special Equipment: *instant-read thermometer*

Remove the pork loin from the refrigerator and let stand
at room temperature for 30 minutes. Preheat the oven to
400 degrees. Place the pork fat side up in a roasting pan
just large enough to hold it.

Combine the garlic, rosemary, lemon zest and fennel seeds
in a food processor or blender and process until coarsely
chopped. Add the olive oil, Dijon mustard, kosher salt and
pepper and process to a smooth paste. Rub the paste over
the pork.

Roast for 1 to 1 1/4 hours or to 160 degrees on an instant-
read thermometer. Remove to a cutting board and tent with
foil. Let stand for 20 minutes before carving.

CHEF'S TIP: Roast chopped fennel with the pork and
serve as a side dish. If the pork loin is an uneven cut, tie
at even intervals with kitchen twine.

Baby Back Ribs

PAIRS WELL WITH SAMUEL ADAMS OCTOBERFEST

SERVES 6

Ribs and Rib Rub

1/4 cup paprika
1/4 cup granulated sugar
2 tablespoons brown sugar
2 tablespoons cumin
2 tablespoons chili powder
2 tablespoons salt
2 tablespoons ground pepper
5 pounds baby back ribs
   (about 3 racks)

Rib Sauce

1 cup smoky barbecue sauce
1/4 cup chopped fresh
   cilantro
3 tablespoons minced red
   onion
2 tablespoons bourbon
2 teaspoons chili powder
3/4 teaspoon ground cumin

Ribs and Rub

Combine the paprika, granulated sugar, brown sugar, cumin,
chili powder, salt and pepper in a bowl; mix well. Rub evenly
over the ribs. Let stand at room temperature for 1 hour.

Preheat the oven to 325 degrees. Place the ribs bone side
up on a rack in a shallow roasting pan. Roast for 2 hours
without turning.

Sauce

Combine the barbecue sauce, cilantro, onion, bourbon,
chili powder and cumin in a small heavy saucepan; mix well.
Bring to a boil over medium heat, stirring occasionally. Brush
over the ribs to serve. Bring the remaining sauce to a boil and
serve with the ribs.

CHEF'S TIP: To finish the ribs on a hot grill, brush with
the barbecue sauce and grill 4 inches from the heat source
for 3 minutes on each side, turning and brushing with the
sauce frequently.

Bacon-Wrapped Pork Tenderloin

Courtesy of Chef and Partner Mark Dommen, One Market Restaurant

PAIRS WELL WITH PLUMPJACK SYRAH

SERVES 4 TO 6

Apple Cider Sauce

8 cups (¹/2 gallon) apple cider
2 tablespoons butter
Sea salt and freshly ground pepper to taste
Cider vinegar to taste

Pork Tenderloin

2 (1-pound) pork tenderloins
Sea salt and freshly ground pepper to taste
8 ounces thinly sliced applewood-smoked bacon
2 tablespoons grapeseed oil

Caramelized Apples

2 Fuji apples, peeled and cored
¹/4 cup grapeseed oil

Creamed Dandelion Greens

4 garlic cloves
1 tablespoon grapeseed oil
¹/4 cup cream
Sea salt to taste
1 bunch dandelion greens (see right)
1 large shallot, chopped
1 tablespoon butter
Freshly ground pepper to taste

Sauce

Bring the apple cider to a boil over high heat. Cook until reduced to 1 cup. Whisk in the butter and season with sea salt and pepper. Add cider vinegar if needed to balance the sweetness.

Tenderloin

Preheat the oven to 400 degrees. Trim the pork of fat and silver skin. Start at the tail end and make a horizontal cut about one-third of the way up, cutting three-fourths of the way through each tenderloin; fold the tail under to make an even fillet. Season with sea salt and pepper. Arrange half the bacon in overlapping layers on plastic wrap. Place one tenderloin on the bacon and use the plastic wrap as a guide to roll, enclosing the pork completely with the bacon. Repeat with the remaining bacon and pork. Season with sea salt and pepper. Sear the tenderloins in the grapeseed oil in a heated sauté pan for 2 minutes on each side. Remove to a rack in a roasting pan and roast for 18 to 20 minutes or until cooked medium. Let rest in a warm place for 10 minutes before carving.

Apples

Cut the apples into twelve circles. Sauté in the grapeseed oil in a heated sauté pan until caramelized. Drain on paper towels. Keep warm in the oven.

Dandelion Greens

Blanch the garlic three times in clean water in a small saucepan to soften; drain. Sauté the garlic in the grapeseed oil in a small sauté pan over medium-high heat until light brown. Add the cream and cook until reduced by half. Process in a blender until smooth. Bring a large saucepan of water to a boil and add enough sea salt to make it as salty as sea water. Add the dandelion greens and blanch. Remove to ice water to stop the cooking process and press to remove as much water as possible; chop into small pieces. Sweat the shallot in the butter in a sauté pan over medium heat until tender. Add the dandelion greens and sauté for several minutes. Stir in the cream sauce and season with sea salt and pepper.

Assembly

Place two apple rings on each plate and top with the creamed dandelion greens. Cut each pork tenderloin into six slices and place on the apple rings. Spoon the cider sauce around the plate.

CHEF'S TIP: You can substitute spinach or Swiss chard for the dandelion greens.

Dandelion Greens

Dandelion greens are the leaves from the plant with yellow flowers that grows wild on lawns; many consider it a weed. The plant is highly nutritious; its long slender leaves have a pleasantly bitter flavor. Look for firm leaves with thin stems and wash thoroughly to remove soil and sand.

THIS PAGE GRACIOUSLY SPONSORED BY ANDREA DEBERRY

Risotto with Sausage and Spinach

PAIRS WELL WITH GLORIA FERRER CARNEROS PINOT NOIR

SERVES 4

2 tablespoons olive oil

1 pound sausage, casings removed and
   sausage crumbled

2 garlic cloves, minced

1 large white onion, chopped

1 large red bell pepper, chopped

1 1/2 cups arborio rice

6 cups chicken broth, heated

2 cups fresh spinach leaves

1/4 cup (1 ounce) grated Parmesan cheese

Salt and freshly ground pepper to taste

Heat the olive oil in a Dutch oven or large heavy saucepan over medium heat. Add the sausage and sauté for 5 minutes or until brown. Remove the sausage with a slotted spoon and drain on paper towels. Drain the Dutch oven, leaving 1/4 cup olive oil in the pan.

Sauté the garlic in the reserved olive oil for 1 minute or until fragrant. Add the onion and bell pepper and sauté for 5 minutes or until the onion is tender. Stir in the rice and sauté for 2 minutes.

Add 2 cups broth, or enough to cover the rice. Simmer until the broth is absorbed. Add the remaining broth 1 cup at a time, cooking until the broth is absorbed after each addition and the rice is tender, stirring constantly. Add the sausage and cook for 10 minutes longer. Remove from the heat and stir in the spinach and cheese. Season with salt and pepper.

Roasted Cauliflower with Arugula, Prosciutto and Pasta

SERVES 6

4 cups (3/4-inch florets) cauliflower

8 ounces grape tomatoes

1 jalapeño chile, seeded and sliced

3 tablespoons extra-virgin olive oil

1 teaspoon kosher salt

1/4 teaspoon freshly ground pepper

8 large fresh sage leaves

3 garlic cloves

6 ounces prosciutto, sliced

Kosher salt to taste

10 1/2 ounces bow tie pasta

6 ounces baby arugula (about 6 lightly packed cups)

3/4 cup (3 ounces) grated fresh Parmesan cheese

Freshly ground pepper to taste

Preheat the oven to 425 degrees. Toss the cauliflower, tomatoes, jalapeño chile, olive oil, 1 teaspoon kosher salt and 1/4 teaspoon pepper in a large bowl, coating evenly. Spread on a rimmed baking sheet. Roast for 15 minutes or until the cauliflower is golden brown and tender, stirring once or twice. Pulse the sage leaves and garlic in a food processor or blender to mince. Add the prosciutto and pulse until chopped. Mix with the cauliflower on the baking sheet and roast for 5 minutes longer.

Bring a large saucepan of salted water to a boil. Add the pasta and cook al dente. Drain the saucepan, reserving 1/2 cup of the cooking liquid. Combine the pasta with the reserved cooking liquid in the saucepan. Stir in the cauliflower mixture, arugula and cheese. Season with salt and pepper.

Rotolo di Spinaci

SERVES 6

Spinach Filling

4 (10-ounce) packages frozen chopped spinach,
   thawed in the packages
1 cup chopped yellow onion
1/4 cup (1/2 stick) butter
11/2 beef bouillon cubes
1/2 cup (2 ounces) each shredded Swiss cheese, shredded
   Cheddar cheese and grated Gruyèye cheese
8 ounces bacon, crisp-cooked and crumbled

Pasta

2 cups cake flour
1/2 cup (about) all-purpose flour
4 egg yolks
3 tablespoons extra-virgin olive oil
1/2 cup water
1 teaspoon salt
41/2 quarts water
Salt to taste
3 tablespoons butter, softened
1 cup (4 ounces) grated Parmesan cheese
1/2 cup (1 stick) butter, browned

Special Equipment: pasta maker or stand mixer
   with a pasta attachment, cheesecloth, kitchen twine

Filling

Squeeze the spinach to remove some, but not all, of the
liquid. Sauté the onion in the butter in a large skillet over
medium-high heat until wilted and translucent. Add the
spinach and bouillon cubes, mashing the cubes with
a fork. Cook for 20 minutes or until the water is absorbed.
Add the Swiss cheese, Cheddar cheese, Gruyère cheese
and bacon; mix well. Cool to room temperature.

Pasta

Combine the flours, egg yolks, olive oil, water and
1 teaspoon salt in a food processor; mix just until the
dough forms a ball. Knead on a lightly floured surface for
8 minutes or until smooth and elastic, kneading in only
as much additional all-purpose flour as needed to prevent
sticking. Wrap in plastic wrap and let stand at room
temperature for 1 hour.

Run the dough through the finest setting on a pasta maker,
making pasta strips about 4 to 6 inches wide and 20 inches
long. Arrange the strips on a lightly floured cheesecloth and
cover with a cloth to prevent drying out.

Spread the spinach mixture about 1/8 inch thick down the
strips, leaving 1/4-inch borders on the sides and 1-inch
borders at the ends. Roll the strips carefully from the narrow
ends to enclose the filling. Seal the edges with water.

Wrap each roll in a double thickness of cheesecloth and
tie with kitchen twine. Bring the water to a rolling boil in a
large saucepan and season with salt. Add the rolls to the
water and return to a boil. Cook for 15 to 18 minutes. Remove
the rolls to a cutting board. Remove the cheesecloth.

Spread 3 tablespoons butter on a warmed platter. Cut the
rolls into 1/2-inch slices and arrange in overlapping rows on
the platter. Sprinkle with the cheese and drizzle with the
browned butter.

CHEF'S TIP: To brown butter, heat slices of butter in a
stainless steel pan over medium heat. Whisk continuously
as the butter will change color quickly and little brown specks
will appear in the bottom of the pan. The butter is ready
to serve once it has a nice nutty smell and is dark gold.

Desserts

At the dawn of the new millennium, the JLSF continued to fundraise and expand our community programs in groundbreaking ways. The JLSF celebrated ninety years of service to the community. In 2000 we worked to pass a breast cancer treatment bill in the California State Assembly. We also instituted our inaugural Community Leaders Breakfast, a forum where JLSF members, community program representatives, and local and state legislators have the opportunity to collaborate. Home Tour kicked off its tenth anniversary with a Tour d'Elegance theme, held in the Presidio Heights and Presidio Terrace neighborhoods, and realized a record profit of over $180,000. JLSF members approved the development of a Signature Program. The decade also included events with Kids in the Kitchen, a hands-on cooking program for low-income children and their families. The program strives to empower youth to make healthy lifestyle choices, helping to reverse the growth of childhood obesity and its associated health issues.

As for dessert, San Francisco may be best known for its chocolate and ice cream creations. The Ghirardelli chocolate factory, founded in 1852, established itself in the North Point neighborhood at the turn of the twentieth century. Although the chocolate-making operations have since moved to the suburbs, you can still find all varieties of ice cream sundaes and banana splits to share at the North Point location. In 1928, George Whitney invented a favorite local ice cream treat, the It's-It® ice cream sandwich. For several decades, this decadent treat (two oatmeal cookies with vanilla ice cream dipped in chocolate) could be found only at San Francisco's Playland-at-the-Beach amusement park. Today local dessert chefs are making their own ice creams, many flavored by savory herbs and vegetables.

In 2003, San Francisco's Ferry Building, previously used as a bay ferry terminal, re-opened as a marketplace after four years of renovation. It was redesigned to resemble street markets in London and Paris. Coinciding with the city's millennial drive to eat locally and sustainably, the farmers' market at the Ferry Building showcases the best in regional produce, dairy, and meats. In the second half of the decade, Americans showed an interest in local sourcing methods for their food. As a culinary leader, San Francisco hosted the international Slow Food Nation event in 2008.

2000–2010

MEYER LEMON ICE CREAM

Meyer lemons make a refreshing ice cream due to their rich flavor and natural sweetness.

MAKES 4 CUPS

2 cups heavy cream
1/2 cup sugar
Pinch of salt
3 egg yolks
1/2 cup sugar
2 cups milk
Grated zest of 2 Meyer lemons
2/3 cup fresh Meyer lemon juice

Special Equipment: *fine mesh sieve, ice cream freezer*

Mix the cream with 1/2 cup sugar and the salt in a medium saucepan. Bring to a boil over medium heat, stirring occasionally. Let stand at room temperature for 20 minutes.

Whisk the egg yolks with 1/2 cup sugar in a mixing bowl. Add the milk and whisk to mix well. Stir in the lemon zest and add to the cooled cream mixture; mix well. Cook over medium heat for 10 to 15 minutes or until thickened enough to coat the back of a wooden spoon, stirring constantly. Strain through a fine mesh sieve into a bowl. Chill in the refrigerator for 3 hours.

Add the lemon juice and pour into an ice cream freezer. Freeze using the manufacturer's directions.

CHEF'S TIP: If Meyer lemons are not available, substitute regular lemons and add 1 tablespoon fresh orange juice to achieve the Meyer lemon flavor.

Citrus Zesting

Citrus zest adds a bright spark of flavor to a dish. There are special zesters to use for removing the zest from the citrus, but it's hard to go wrong with a fine grater, which produces a light zest that will meld into the dish and give it great flavor. To get the most flavor from the zest, add it toward the end of the cooking time.

STRAWBERRY PARFAITS WITH DATES AND ALMONDS

PAIRS WELL WITH GLORIA FERRER BLANC DE NOIRS

SERVES 4

1/2 cup Medjool dates (4 or 5 dates)
3 pints strawberries
2 teaspoons fresh lemon juice
1/2 cup Medjool dates (4 or 5 dates)
1 1/2 cups raw almonds or pecans
Whipped cream
Mint leaves, for garnish

Special Equipment: *parfait glasses*

Soak 1/2 cup dates with enough warm water to cover in a bowl and let stand for 8 minutes; drain. Reserve 1/2 cup plus four whole strawberries. Cut the remaining strawberries into quarters.

Combine the reserved 1 1/2 cups strawberries with the soaked dates and lemon juice in a blender; process until smooth. Combine with the strawberry quarters in a bowl and mix well.

Combine 1/2 cup dates with the almonds in a food processor and process to the texture of coarse meal.

Alternate layers of the almond mixture and strawberry mixture in parfait glasses, making as many as four layers. Top with whipped cream and garnish with the four reserved whole strawberries and mint leaves. Serve immediately or chill for up to 30 minutes.

THIS PAGE GRACIOUSLY SPONSORED BY TAMMY BRAAS-HILL & RANDOLPH M. HILL

NORTH BEACH TIRAMISU

Recipe originally appeared in San Francisco Flavors, *the third cookbook from* The Junior League of San Francisco, Inc.

SERVES 10 TO 12

48 small ladyfingers or fingers of pound cake
1 cup hot water
2 tablespoons instant espresso powder
1 tablespoon granulated sugar
3 tablespoons light rum or marsala
2 egg yolks
1/4 cup granulated sugar
6 ounces mascarpone cheese or natural
    cream cheese, softened
1 tablespoon fresh lemon juice
1 tablespoon light rum or marsala
1 teaspoon vanilla extract
2 cups heavy whipping cream
1 tablespoon confectioners' sugar
2 egg whites
12 ounces bittersweet chocolate, grated
1/4 cup baking cocoa

Preheat the oven to 325 degrees. Spread the ladyfingers on a baking sheet and toast for 2 to 3 minutes. Cool to room temperature. Combine the hot water, espresso powder and 1 tablespoon granulated sugar in a small bowl and mix well. Stir in 3 tablespoons rum.

Beat the egg yolks with 1/4 cup granulated sugar in a large bowl until the mixture forms a slowly dissolving ribbon on the surface when the beaters are lifted. Blend in the mascarpone cheese with a wooden spoon. Add the lemon juice, 1 tablespoon rum and the vanilla.

Beat the cream with the confectioners' sugar in a large bowl until soft peaks form. Fold into the egg yolk mixture. Beat the egg whites in a large bowl until stiff glossy peaks form. Fold into the cream mixture.

Dip half the ladyfingers one at a time into the espresso mixture; do not soak. Arrange in a 9×13-inch dish. Sprinkle with half the grated chocolate and spread with half the cream mixture. Repeat the layers and dust the top with the baking cocoa. Chill for 4 hours before serving.

CHEF'S TIP: If you are concerned about using raw eggs, use eggs pasteurized in their shells, which are sold at some specialty food stores, or use an equivalent amount of pasteurized egg substitute.

North Beach Tiramisu

North Beach is the Italian enclave in San Francisco, bustling with sidewalk cafés, coffeehouses, and Italian restaurants. Tiramisu is a traditional espresso-soaked dessert layered with a rich mascarpone filling. Buy good-quality ladyfingers or pound cake from a bakery or make your own.

MOLTEN LAVA CHOCOLATE CUPCAKES

Courtesy of Chef Michael Chiarello, Napa Style and Bottega

SERVES 12

1/4 cup baking cocoa
8 ounces bittersweet chocolate
1/2 cup (1 stick) unsalted butter, softened
1 cup heavy cream
4 eggs, at room temperature
1 1/3 cups granulated sugar
1/2 cup mayonnaise
1/2 cup cornstarch
1/2 teaspoon cinnamon
1/2 teaspoon finely ground gray sea salt or white sea salt
Confectioners' sugar

Preheat the oven to 300 degrees. Place muffin pans on baking sheets and heat in the oven for 5 minutes. Spray the muffin cups with nonstick cooking spray and dust with the baking cocoa; tap out the excess baking cocoa.

Use a large knife to shave 5 ounces of the chocolate into thin slivers in a heatproof bowl. Cut the remaining 3 ounces chocolate into twelve chunks and reserve. Combine the butter and cream in a small saucepan over medium-high heat. Bring to a simmer. Pour over the shaved chocolate and mix gently to melt and blend.

Whisk the eggs with the granulated sugar, mayonnaise, cornstarch, cinnamon and sea salt in a bowl until the sugar has dissolved. Add the melted chocolate mixture and mix gently; overmixing will prevent the cupcakes from rising. Scoop by 1/4 cupfuls into the prepared muffin cups, filling three-fourths full.

Bake for 40 to 50 minutes or just until a wooden pick inserted into the center comes out clean. Press one reserved chocolate chunk gently into the center of each cupcake while still hot; a crust will form if this is not done while the cupcake is hot and you will spoil the appearance.

Cool in the muffin pans for 10 minutes. Remove to a wire rack and dust with confectioners' sugar.

CHEF'S TIP: The mayonnaise will add moisture to the cake. It can be omitted without adjusting the recipe, but it has an amazing effect.

THIS PAGE GRACIOUSLY SPONSORED BY MERRILL KASPER, LAURA SCHAFER & TRISH OTSTOTT

FRUIT PIZZA

The vibrant colors of this dish never fail to provide the "Wow" factor. This is an easy recipe that is fun to make with children because they can do most of the work.

SERVES 10 TO 12

Fruit Pizza Crust

1 1/4 cups plus 2 tablespoons all-purpose flour
1 teaspoon cream of tartar
1/2 teaspoon baking soda
1/8 teaspoon salt
1/2 cup (1 stick) unsalted butter, softened
3/4 cup sugar
1 egg

Pizza

8 ounces fruit-flavored yogurt
1 large banana, sliced
Juice of 1 lemon
4 kiwifruit, peeled and sliced
5 ounces raspberries
2 1/2 ounces blackberries
2 large strawberries, cut into halves

Special Equipment: *round 13-inch pizza pan*

Crust

Preheat the oven to 400 degrees and place a rack in the center of the oven. Combine the flour, cream of tartar, baking soda and salt in a bowl and mix with a fork.

Cream the butter and sugar at high speed in a mixing bowl until light and fluffy. Beat in the egg just until blended. Add the dry ingredients gradually, beating at low speed to form a smooth dough.

Spread the dough on a round 13-inch pizza pan. Bake for 10 to 12 minutes or until the crust is golden brown around the edge. Cool to room temperature.

Pizza

Spread the yogurt on the cooled crust. Toss the banana with the lemon juice in a bowl to prevent browning. Arrange the kiwifruit around the outer edge of the crust. Add circles of the raspberries, banana and blackberries and place the strawberries in the center. Cut into wedges to serve.

CHEF'S TIP: Seasonal fruit is best; experiment with what is fresh. You can prepare and store the pizza for up to 1 day in the refrigerator before the crust loses its crispness.

SEASONAL FRUIT COBBLER

SERVES 12 TO 16

1/2 cup (1 stick) butter, melted
1 cup all-purpose flour
1 cup sugar
1 tablespoon baking powder
Pinch of salt
1 cup milk
1/2 teaspoon vanilla extract
5 or 6 peaches, peeled and thinly sliced (about 4 cups)
1 cup sugar
1 tablespoon fresh lemon juice
1 teaspoon ground cinnamon
1/4 teaspoon ground nutmeg

Preheat the oven to 375 degrees. Spread the butter in a 9×13-inch baking dish. Mix the flour with 1 cup sugar, the baking powder and salt in a medium bowl. Add the milk and vanilla and mix just until combined. Pour in the prepared baking dish; do not stir.

Combine the peaches, 1 cup sugar, the lemon juice, cinnamon and nutmeg in a small saucepan and bring to a boil over high heat, stirring constantly. Boil for 1 to 2 minutes. Spoon over the batter in the baking dish. Bake for 40 to 45 minutes or until the crust is golden brown. Serve warm or cold.

THIS PAGE GRACIOUSLY SPONSORED BY EVE WERTSCH

APPLE CRISP

PAIRS WELL WITH GLORIA FERRER VA DE VI

SERVES 4

3/4 cup all-purpose flour

1/4 cup packed light brown sugar

2 tablespoons granulated sugar

1/2 teaspoon salt

1/2 cup (1 stick) unsalted butter, softened

1 cup rolled oats

2 large or 3 small Granny Smith apples, peeled and
    coarsely chopped

2 large or 3 small Fuji apples, peeled and
    coarsely chopped

1/4 cup golden raisins (optional)

1/4 cup slivered almonds or chopped walnuts (optional)

1/2 cup granulated sugar

1 tablespoon lemon juice

1 tablespoon orange juice

1/2 teaspoon ground cinnamon or pumpkin pie spice

Mix the flour, brown sugar, 2 tablespoons granulated sugar and the salt in a large bowl. Combine with the butter in a food processor and pulse until the texture of coarse meal; you can also mix with a pastry blender. Add the oats and mix with your fingers to form large moist clumps. Chill in the freezer.

Preheat the oven to 375 degrees. Toss the apples with the raisins, almonds, 1/2 cup granulated sugar, the lemon juice, orange juice and cinnamon in a large bowl. Spoon into a 2-quart baking dish and top with the oats mixture.

Place on a rimmed baking sheet and bake for 55 to 65 minutes or until golden brown and bubbly. Cool for 10 minutes. Serve with vanilla ice cream or frozen yogurt.

Gloria Ferrer's Pinot Noir-Inspired Sparkling Wines

Gloria Ferrer's sparkling wines are defined by a commitment to pinot noir, which adds longevity, beauty, and a delicate combination of aromas, flavors, and mouthfeel to seven distinctly different sparkling wines. Experience the delicate balance that makes pinot noir famous for food pairing in each of these versatile sparkling wines for yourself, with Sonoma Brut, Blanc de Noirs, Va di Vi, Blanc de Blancs, Royal Cuvée, Brut Rosé, and the tête de cuvée Carneros Cuvée.

Chocolate Macadamia Nut Pie

This rich and velvety pie is great served warm or at room temperature.

SERVES 8

Coffee Liqueur Whipped Cream
1 cup heavy whipping cream
2 tablespoons sugar
1 tablespoon coffee liqueur

Pie
1/4 cup (1/2 stick) butter, melted
1 1/4 cups sugar
1/4 cup baking cocoa
3 eggs, lightly beaten
1 (5-ounce) can evaporated milk
1/4 cup coffee liqueur
1/4 teaspoon salt
3/4 cup chopped macadamia nuts
1 baked (9-inch) pie shell

Whipped Cream
Beat the cream at high speed in a medium mixing bowl until it begins to thicken. Add the sugar and liqueur and beat until firm peaks form. Chill for 8 to 12 hours.

Pie
Preheat the oven to 350 degrees. Blend the butter with the sugar and baking cocoa in a mixing bowl. Add the eggs and beat for 2 minutes. Beat in the evaporated milk, coffee liqueur and salt. Stir in the macadamia nuts. Spoon into the pie shell and cover with a pie crust guard or foil to prevent burning.

Bake for 40 to 45 minutes or until the edge is set and the center shakes slightly when gently shaken. Cool for 1 1/2 hours or longer. Cut the pie into wedges and top with the whipped cream.

THIS PAGE GRACIOUSLY SPONSORED BY ANNE MARIE MASSOCCA

Pastel de Tres Leches

SERVES 18

Cake

2 cups all-purpose flour
2 tablespoons baking powder
1/2 teaspoon salt
8 eggs
2 cups sugar
6 tablespoons water
2 tablespoons vanilla extract

Tres Leches

1 (14-ounce) can sweetened condensed milk
1 (10-ounce) can evaporated milk
2 cups heavy cream
3 tablespoons whole milk

Meringue Topping

1 egg white
1 cup sugar
1/2 teaspoon cream of tartar
1/2 teaspoon vanilla extract
1/4 teaspoon white vinegar
Pinch of salt
1/2 cup boiling water
Fresh raspberries, for garnish

Cake

Preheat the oven to 325 degrees. Mix the flour, baking powder and salt together. Beat the eggs in a mixing bowl until thick and foamy. Add the sugar gradually, beating constantly. Add the flour mixture alternately with the water, mixing well after each addition. Mix in the vanilla.

Spoon into a greased 9×13-inch baking dish and bake for 20 minutes or until golden brown. Cool in the baking dish on a wire rack for 15 minutes. Punch holes in the cake with a skewer.

Tres Leches

Combine the sweetened condensed milk, evaporated milk, cream and whole milk in a blender and process just until well mixed. Pour over the cake. Cover and chill in the refrigerator for 3 to 4 hours.

Topping

Combine the egg white, sugar, cream of tartar, vanilla, vinegar and salt in a mixing bowl. Set at high speed and immediately add the boiling water. Beat until soft peaks form. Spoon over the cake and garnish servings with raspberries.

BLACKBERRY CORNMEAL CAKE

This cake tastes even better the next day and is delicious served at room temperature.

SERVES 8 TO 10

Blackberry Cake

2 cups fresh blackberries
2 tablespoons all-purpose flour
2 tablespoons sugar
1 1/3 cups all-purpose flour
1/4 cup finely ground cornmeal
1 teaspoon baking powder
1/2 teaspoon kosher salt
6 tablespoons unsalted butter, at room temperature
1 cup sugar
1 teaspoon finely grated lemon zest
2 eggs
1 tablespoon lemon juice
1 teaspoon almond extract
1/2 cup milk

Whipped Cream

1 cup heavy whipping cream
1 teaspoon sugar
1 teaspoon vanilla extract

Special Equipment: *stand mixer with paddle and whisk attachments*

Cake

Toss the blackberries with 2 tablespoons flour and 2 tablespoons sugar in a bowl, coating evenly and mashing lightly; the berries should retain their shape but begin to release their juices.

Preheat the oven to 350 degrees and place the oven rack in the center of the oven. Butter a round 9-inch cake pan and line with baking parchment. Butter and lightly flour the parchment, tapping out the excess flour.

Whisk 1 1/3 cups flour with the cornmeal, baking powder and kosher salt in a medium bowl. Cream the butter with 1 cup sugar and the lemon zest in a stand mixer with a paddle attachment on medium-high for 3 minutes or until light and fluffy. Reduce the speed to medium and blend in one of the eggs for 20 seconds. Beat in the remaining egg, the lemon juice and almond extract. Fold in half the flour mixture with a spatula. Fold in the milk and remaining flour mixture. Spread evenly in the prepared cake pan.

Bake for 15 minutes. Scatter the blackberries quickly over the top and bake for 20 to 25 minutes longer or until a wooden pick inserted into the center comes out clean. Cool on a wire rack for 15 to 30 minutes. Invert the cake onto the wire rack. Remove the baking parchment and invert the cake onto a serving plate.

Whipped Cream

Combine the whipping cream, sugar and vanilla in a stand mixer with a whisk attachment. Beat at high speed until soft peaks form. Store in the refrigerator until needed. Serve over the cake.

Ancho Chile Brownies

PAIRS WELL WITH ROSATI FAMILY WINERY CABERNET SAUVIGNON, MENDOCINO COUNTY

MAKES 16

6 tablespoons unsalted butter

4 ounces (68% cacao) TCHOPro Baking Drops or
   bittersweet chocolate

1 tablespoon baking cocoa

2 tablespoons vegetable oil

3/4 cup packed brown sugar

1/4 cup granulated sugar

3 eggs

1 teaspoon vanilla extract

3/4 cup unbleached flour

3 tablespoons ancho chile powder

1 teaspoon cinnamon

1/4 teaspoon salt

1 cup (6 ounces) semisweet chocolate chips or miniature
   semisweet chocolate chips

Preheat the oven to 350 degrees. Place the butter, baking drops and baking cocoa in a double boiler. Heat over simmering water until the butter and chocolate melt, stirring to blend well. Remove from the heat and stir in the oil, brown sugar and granulated sugar.

Whisk in the eggs quickly and then the vanilla. Fold in the flour, chile powder, cinnamon and salt. Add the chocolate chips and mix just until incorporated. Spread in an 8×8-inch baking pan sprayed with nonstick cooking spray. Bake for 25 to 30 minutes or until a wooden pick inserted into the center comes out clean. Cool on a wire rack and cut into squares to serve.

CHEF'S TIP: You can speed up the preparation time by using the microwave instead of a double boiler. Place the butter, baking drops, and baking cocoa in a microwave-safe dish and microwave for 30 seconds; stir. Microwave in 30-second intervals until the butter and chocolate melt, stirring after each interval.

CHOCOLATE AND PEANUT BUTTER SQUARES

MAKES 12 TO 16

2 1/2 cups all-purpose flour
2 teaspoons baking soda
1 teaspoon salt
1 cup (2 sticks) butter, softened
1 cup crunchy peanut butter
1 cup packed brown sugar
1 cup granulated sugar
2 eggs
2 teaspoons vanilla extract
8 ounces chocolate chips
5 ounces peanut butter chips

Preheat the oven to 375 degrees. Sift the flour, baking soda and salt into a medium bowl. Beat the butter and peanut butter in a large bowl until well mixed. Add the brown sugar and granulated sugar and beat until light and fluffy. Beat in the eggs and vanilla. Stir in the flour mixture. Fold in the chocolate chips and peanut butter chips.

Spoon into a greased 9×13-inch baking dish. Bake for 15 minutes or until light brown. Cool slightly on a wire rack and cut into squares to serve.

Triple-Chip Cookies

MAKES 36

1 cup plus 2 tablespoons all-purpose flour
1/2 teaspoon baking soda
1/2 cup (1 stick) unsalted butter, softened
1/2 cup granulated sugar
1/2 cup packed light brown sugar
1 egg
1 1/2 teaspoons vanilla extract
1/4 teaspoon salt
*1/2 cup (60.5% cacao) TCHOPro Baking Drops or
   semisweet chocolate chips*
1/2 cup butterscotch chips
1/2 cup peanut butter chips

Preheat the oven to 375 degrees. Place an oven rack in the center of the oven. Whisk the flour and baking soda together.

Cream the butter with the granulated sugar and brown sugar at medium speed in a mixing bowl until light and fluffy. Beat in the egg, vanilla and salt. Stir in the flour mixture. Add the baking drops, butterscotch chips and peanut butter chips; mix well.

Drop by large spoonfuls several inches apart onto a greased cookie sheet. Bake for 8 to 10 minutes or until light brown on top with brown edges. Cool on the baking sheet on a wire rack for 2 minutes. Remove to the wire rack to cool completely.

Perfectly Round Cookies

Professional bakers create perfectly round cookies every time by using simple tools that you probably own too, such as an ice cream scoop or large melon ball scoop. The uniform dough size creates uniform cookies for even and consistent baking and a professional look.

THIS PAGE GRACIOUSLY SPONSORED BY JEAN & JEFF PEDIGO

GINGER THINS

MAKES 18 TO 24

2 teaspoons baking soda
1 tablespoon hot water
3 cups all-purpose flour
2 teaspoons ground cinnamon
1 teaspoon ground ginger
1/2 teaspoon ground cloves
1 cup (2 sticks) butter, softened
1 1/2 cups sugar
2 teaspoons dark corn syrup
1 egg, lightly beaten

Dissolve the baking soda in the hot water in a small cup. Sift the flour, cinnamon, ginger and cloves into a large bowl. Cream the butter and sugar at high speed in a mixing bowl until light and fluffy. Add the corn syrup, egg and baking soda mixture; mix well. Blend in the flour mixture to form a dough. Chill for 2 to 3 hours.

Preheat the oven to 375 degrees. Roll the dough very thin on a lightly floured surface. Cut with cookie cutters and place on an ungreased cookie sheet. Bake for 8 to 10 minutes or until golden brown. Remove to a wire rack to cool.

CHEF'S TIP: Cookie cutters can also be used as cute napkin rings.

BROWN SUGAR AND ALMOND BISCOTTI

MAKES ABOUT 30

3 1/4 cups all-purpose flour
1 1/4 cups packed light brown sugar
1 cup plus 2 tablespoons granulated sugar
1 1/2 teaspoons baking powder
1 teaspoon salt
3 eggs
1/2 cup (1 stick) unsalted butter, melted
2 teaspoons almond extract
1 teaspoon vanilla extract
1 1/2 cups slivered almonds

Preheat the oven to 300 degrees. Whisk the flour with the brown sugar, granulated sugar, baking powder and salt in a bowl. Combine the eggs, butter and extracts in a bowl and whisk until smooth. Stir in the almonds. Stir into the flour mixture; mix well.

Knead lightly on a lightly floured surface until the mixture forms a dough. Shape into two 4×10-inch logs with moistened fingers. Place on baking sheets lined with baking parchment. Bake for 45 minutes or until firm and golden brown.

Reduce the oven temperature to 250 degrees. Cool the logs on the baking sheets for 10 minutes. Remove to a cutting board and remove the baking parchment from the baking sheets. Cut the logs diagonally into 3/4-inch slices with a serrated knife. Arrange cut side down on the baking sheets. Bake for 15 minutes on each side or until dry.

Sponsors

Lombard Street

Gloria Ferrer Caves and Vineyards
gloriaferrer.com
Sonoma, California

Cable Car

The Boston Beer Company
Brewers of Samuel Adams Beer
samueladams.com
Boston, Massachusetts

Union Square

Acorn Winery/Alegria Vineyards
Betsy & Bill Nachbaur
acornwinery.com
Healdsburg, California

Blackbird Vineyards
blackbirdvineyards.com
Napa, California

Blue Angel Vodka
blueangelvodka.com
San Francisco, California

Boudin Bakery
boudinbakery.com
San Francisco, California

Dane Cellars
danecellars.com
Vineburg, California

Dolce Winery
dolcewine.com
Oakville, California

Emile Henry
emilehenryusa.com

Far Niente Winery
farniente.com
Oakville, California

Honig Vineyards and Winery
honigwine.com
Rutherford, California

Julia Morgan Ballroom
juliamorganballroom.com
San Francisco, California

Lara Hata: Photographer
larahata.com
San Francisco, California

Liza Gershman Photography
lizagershman.com
San Francisco, California

Matthew Washburn—Photographer
washburnimagery.com
San Francisco, California

Mazzocco Sonoma Winery
mazzocco.com
Healdsburg, California

Pacific Digital Image
pacdigital.com
San Francisco, California

Rosati Family Winery
rosatifamilywines.com
Mendocino County, California

Nickel and Nickel Vineyards
nickelandnickel.com
Oakville, California

PlumpJack
plumpjackwinery.com
Oakville, California

TCHO Chocolate
tcho.com
San Francisco, California

CRISSY FIELD

Kenneth Aguilar & Kendi Aguilar
Wendy Simon Armstrong & Benton Armstrong
Courtney & Nick Bocci
Katie Borzcik
Sara & Paul Borzcik
Tammy Braas-Hill & Randolph M. Hill
Michelle Nicole Branch
Cici & Whitney Hoover
Usha Burns & Joanne Horning
Kathryn & Peter Colosi
Andrea DeBerry
Hillary Homs
Jennifer L. Johnston
Beth & Fred Karren
Leslie Karren
Merrill Kasper, Laura Schafer & Trish Otstott
Christine & Dustin Keele

Jennifer Kurrie
Anne Marie Massocca
Irena Matijas
Michelle & Kristian McCabe
Shannon Murphy & Murphy Family
Amy Nichols
Kimberly & Colin O'Connell
Suzy Pak & Mark Gundacker
Robyn & Ron Pawlo
Jean & Jeff Pedigo
Amie Pfeifer
Bichhope & Co Phan
Lillian Phan
Dariana & Mason Ross
Eve Wertsch
Lindsey & Jonathan Wetzel
Amanda Willson

Acknowledgments

WINE EXPERT ACKNOWLEDGMENTS

Ainsley Hines
WSET Master of Wine

Chef Taylor Mason, Private Chef and Wine Consultant
Chef of Ma(i)sonry Napa Valley, Yountville, California

Tommy Ronquillo, Certified Sommelier
Vinos Unico Importers, San Francisco

RECIPE ACKNOWLEDGMENTS

Bottega
Chef Michael Chiarello
botteganapavalley.com
Yountville, California

The Buena Vista
thebuenavista.com
Fisherman's Wharf, San Francisco, California

Chef Laurie Gauguin
Private Chef
San Francisco, California

Hands On Gourmet
Chef Stephen Gibbs
handsongourmet.com
San Francisco, California

Fifth Floor
Chef Jennie Lorenzo
fifthfloorrestaurant.com
Union Square, San Francisco, California

Franciscan Crab
Chef Andrea Froncillo
franciscanrestaurant.com
Fisherman's Wharf, San Francisco, California

Gather
Chef Sean Baker
gatherrestaurant.com
Berkeley, California

Greens Restaurant
Executive Chef Annie Somerville
greensrestaurant.com
Fort Mason, San Francisco, California

Madrona Manor
Executive Chef Jesse Mallgren
madronamanor.com
Healdsburg, California

One Market Restaurant
Chef and Partner Mark Dommen
onemarket.com
Financial District, San Francisco, California

Oola Restaurant and Bar
oola-sf.com
SOMA, San Francisco, California

Piperade
Chef Gerald Hirigoyen
piperade.com
Embarcadero, San Francisco, California

Pisco Latin Lounge
Chef/Owner James Schenk
piscosf.com
Castro, San Francisco, California

Restaurant Gary Danko
Chef Gary Danko
garydanko.com
Fisherman's Wharf, San Francisco, California

Rose Pistola
Chef Pablo Estrada
rosepistola.com
North Beach, San Francisco, California

Rose's Café
Chef Mark Gordon
rosescafesf.com
Cow Hollow, San Francisco, California

Ryan Scott 2 Go
Chef Ryan Scott
ryanscott2go.com
San Francisco, California

Swan Oyster Depot
Nob Hill, San Francisco, California

Terzo
Chef Mark Gordon
terzosf.com
Cow Hollow, San Francisco, California

The Tipsy Pig
thetipsypigsf.com
Marina, San Francisco, California

Williams-Sonoma
Founder Chuck Williams
williams-sonoma.com
Union Square, San Francisco, California

Cookbook Committees

2007–2009 PLANNING COMMITTEE

Katie Borzcik, *Committee Chair*

Suanne Bouvier	Adele du Tertre	Shannon Murphy
Tammy Braas-Hill	Catherine Fischer	Michelle Seith
Heather Bryce	Cynthia Foster	Angela Tortorici
Usha Burns	Christine Kaddaras	Jenna Wrobel

2009–2010 DEVELOPMENT COMMITTEE

Katie Borzcik, *Committee Chair*
Michelle McCabe, *Recipe Development Chair*
Shannon Murphy, *Marketing & Underwriting Chair*

Tammy Braas-Hill	Joanne Horning	Amie Pfeifer
Usha Burns	Leslie Karren	Lillian Phan
Katie Colosi	Christine Keele	Najwa Smith-Schmookler
Catherine Fischer	Amy Nichols	Lindsey Wetzel
Cynthia Foster		Jenna Wrobel

2010–2011 Launch Committee

Katie Borzcik, *Committee Chair*
Michelle McCabe, *Launch Party Chair*
Shannon Murphy, *Sales & Marketing Chair*
Amy Nichols, *Public Relations Chair*

Brittney Beck
Christy Bonner
Tammy Braas-Hill
Michelle Branch
Usha Burns
Kathryn Cavanaugh
Katie Colosi
Amy Dawson
Tegan Firth

Catherine Fischer
Cynthia Foster
Renee Goldstein
Joanne Horning
Jennifer Johnston
Leslie Karren
Cora McAlpine
Courtney McSpadden

Molly K. Myers
Amber Overholser
Amie Pfeifer
Amanda Rickel
Auben Salazar
Cristina Serafyn
Carla Vaccarezza
Lindsey Wetzel
Jenna Wrobel

League Presidents

2007–2008
Stacey Fleece

2008–2010
Gwinneth Berexa

2010–2011
Cynthia Wolfe Funai

Tasting Committee

Laila Abdul
Kendi Aguilar
Kelly Anderson
Jennifer Andresen
Elizabeth Arbuckle
Wendy Simon Armstrong
Jennifer Axcell
Julianne Baker
Brittany Barr
Blossom Barnes
Alana Barrett
Elizabeth Bearden
Caitlin Jane Berry
Neria Blanquera
Erika Lodge Boissiere
Erin Boldt
Katie Borzcik
Tammy Braas-Hill
Lauren Bradley
Brigid Brady
Michelle Branch
Rebecca Brownlee
Becky Bruno
Usha Burns
Alicia Burt
Dewi Burton

Erin Bushell
Kim Byrne
Kathryn Cavanaugh
Adaire Chamyan
Jacquelynne Chimera
Carrie Colla
Katie Colosi
Courtney Comb
Kelly Crisp
Jen Cronan
Emily de Ayora
Jill Diaforli
Jennifer Ellison
Jennifer Erickson
Sara Farner
Tegan Firth
Mary Florcruz
Cynthia Foster
Alexa Fox
Andrea Ghoorah-Sieminski
Merrill Gillespie
Renee Goldstein
Priya Gopinath
Heidi Gorrebeeck
Catherine Gravelle
Kristyn Greene

Jennifer Hart
Katie Hendrix
Hillary Homs
Whitney Hoover
Joanne Horning
Jessica Hoyt
Alyson Huff
Kelly Jacikas
Alexandra Jamieson
Meghan Jenkins
Jennifer Johnston
Yuri Kanno
Leslie Karren
Christine Keele
Myka Keil
Maureen Kennelly
Lisa Kitchen
Brooke Kruger
Dariana Lau
Margaret Lilani
Caroline Linton
Elizabeth Little
Alexandra Loginoff
Catherine Longworth
Mimi Luong
Alexandra MacRae

Elizabeth Majoch
Lisa Masters
Michelle McCabe
Shelby McKinley
Amanda McNeil
Vanessa Mendoza
Natasha Merritt
Kelly Miller
Julie Milleson
Elizabeth Mitsky
Marianne Moser
Shannon Murphy
Molly K. Myers
Amy Nichols
Angela Nicolella
Theresa Nicoletto
Lindsay Noren
Naomi Obana
Kimberly O'Connell
Melanie Ogren
Briana Olson
Yassi Oreyzi
Kenzi Parton
Robyn Pawlo
Sara Pelosi
Amie Pfeifer

Lillian Phan
Sarah Pinto
Melissa Powar
Megan Purdy
Melissa Quigg
Carolyn Raine
Emilie Rekart
Amanda Rickel
Courtney Risman-Jones
Molly Rogers
Amy Roither
Kelly Russell
Auben Salazr
Rachel Samuels
Lisa Schwartz
Sarah Semple
Cristina Serafyn
Madyé Y. Seymour
Anne Sissel
Leigh Sitzman
Kirsten Sloneker
Najwa Smith-Schmookler
Rebecca Stamey-White
Kat Stark
Jennifer Strassburger
Kate Sullivan

Candace Tam
Jessica Tankersley
Devon Tarasevic
Christina Torres
Linda Tucei
Erin Tulley
Mary Turnipseed
Carla Vaccarezza
Amanda Valentino
Anne Walbridge
Stephanie Wang
Michelle Wangler
Emily Watson
Erin Wermuth
Lindsey Wetzel
Amy Whalen
Victoria Wild
Amanda Willson
Courtney Wilson
Ashley Wood
Jennifer Young

Recipe Contributors

The following members of The Junior League of San Francisco submitted more than 500 recipes on behalf of their friends, families, and colleagues. Thank you for making our cookbook a success!

Adriana Abbe	Sara Farner	Tam Madden	Melissa Powar
Kendi Aguilar	Tegan Firth	Stephanie Martin	Megan Purdy
Kelly Anderson	Catherine Fischer	Lisa Masters	Merrill Reardon
Kris Anthony	Cynthia Foster	Michelle McCabe	Amanda Rickel
Elizabeth Arbuckle	Andrea Ghoorah-Sieminski	Kelly McRory	Courtney Risman-Jones
Wendy Simon Armstrong	Renee Goldstein	Natasha Merritt	Michel Rossano
Jennifer Axcell	Lauren Haswell	Elizabeth Mitsky	Kelly Russell
Blossom Barnes	Hillary Homs	Marlene Moffitt	Leslie Ryder
Nicole Bonar	Joanne Horning	Whitney Morgan	Auben Salazar
Jamie Bordewyk	Schuyler Hudak	Claire Morris	Rachel Samuels
Katie Borzcik	Alyson Huff	Maryellen P. Mullin	Lisa Schwartz
Tammy Braas-Hill	Alexandra Jamieson	Shannon Murphy	Sarah Semple
Brigid Brady	Jennifer Johnston	Molly K. Myers	Cristina Serafyn
Michelle Branch	Yuri Kanno	Amy Nichols	Madyé Y. Seymour
Becky Bruno	Leslie Karren	Kimberly O'Connell	Najwa Smith-Schmookler
Kim Byrne	Christine Keele	Laura O'Donnell	Kate Sullivan
Beth Catcher	Myka Keil	Melanie Ogren	Devon Tarasevic
Kathryn Cavanaugh	Kris Kolassa	Yassi Oreyzi	Kim Toney
Dolly Chammas	Brooke Kruger	Jenny Osman	Mary Turnipseed
Adaire Chamyan	Dariana Lau	Robyn Pawlo	Katie Tuttle
Jacquelynne Chimera	Margaret Lilani	Janna Pellegrino	Amanda Valentino
Lauren Cohn	Melissa Lindia	Camille Perrine	Lindsey Wetzel
Katie Colosi	Elizabeth Little	Amie Pfeifer	Erica Whitaker
Jen Cronan	Lindsay Lockwood	Lillian Phan	Amanda Willson
Jennifer Ellison	Zuzy Martin Lynch	Sarah Pinto	

Index

For additional copies of

SAN FRANCISCO
Entertains

A Cookbook Celebrating the Centennial
of The Junior League of San Francisco, Inc.

Please contact
The Junior League of San Francisco, Inc.
2226A Fillmore Street
San Francisco, California 94115
415-775-4100
www.jlsf.org